UNCLE TOM AT WAR
FROM PENMACHNO TO PRISON CAMP

Uncle Tom at War

From Penmachno to Prison Camp

Hywel Roberts

To my grandchildren,
Cara, Seán and Calan,
in order that they can learn
about this part of their heritage,

and also to my wife
Margaret
for her support
and enormous patience.

First published in 2014

© Hywel Roberts

© Gwasg Carreg Gwalch 2014

ISBN: 978-1-84524-224-4

Cover design: Eleri Owen

Published by Gwasg Carreg Gwalch,
12 Iard yr Orsaf, Llanrwst, Wales LL26 0EH
tel: 01492 642031
fax: 01492 641502
email: books@carreg-gwalch.com
website: www.carreg-gwalch.com

Contents

Foreword

This is a book about the life of my grandfather's brother Tom, but the Great War is a major feature of the story. It was a remarkable chance meeting in the Penmachno churchyard in 2002 that inspired me to start researching my family history, and I then started giving talks to family history and other societies. I now have eight talks in my family history saga and Tom's story is only one. But there's a huge difference between preparing a talk and writing a book! In addition to the family history, I've tried to provide a summary of the activities of the Liverpool Scottish during the war, the war in general and particularly the treatment of prisoners of war. I've also been able to include a summary of another prisoner's POW diary and some interesting documents issued to prisoners. I would like to thank a number of people who have been particularly helpful.

I'm truly grateful for the support received from The Liverpool Scottish Museum Trust, in particular the Secretary, Major Ian Riley, and the Archivist, Dennis Reeves, both of whom have provided information, documents and advice. They gave permission to publish the 'Beer Garden' and 'Eisteddfod' posters, together with the Chavasse photos in Chapter 7.

The newspaper reports on my grandfather's Tribunal appearances in Chapter 3 were provided by my friend Vivian Parry Williams. Vivian is a prominent local historian who has assisted me with several aspects of family history research. He has published *Hanes Plwyf Penmachno* ('the history of Penmachno parish'), and also *Owen Gethin Jones – Ei Fywyd a'i Feiau*, both published by Carreg Gwalch.

Permission to publish the two maps of the Battle of Cambrai (Chapter 8) was given by Chris Baker, the person responsible for 'The Long, Long Trail' (see *www.1914-18.net*). Permission to publish the 'Map of the main prison camps in Germany and Austria' was given by the National Archives.

In Chapter 9 permission to publish the hymn tune 'Preswylfa' was given by my friend Arthur Morgan Thomas, grandson of the composer Robert Richard Thomas.

Chapter 10 has been made possible because of the kindness of two people. Permission to include extracts from the War Diary of Sergeant James Cunningham was given by his grandson, James Cunningham of Dunfermline. Permission to provide a copy of the Berlin declaration made on 11 November 1918 and the leaflet given to prisoners leaving the Cassel POW Camp was given by Richard Lloyd of Birmingham.

Hywel Roberts
June 2014

1
1800-1904
Uncle Tom's Family

Thomas Williams was part of a family with deep roots in the village of Penmachno, in the Machno valley about 5 miles south of Betws y Coed in the Conwy valley in northern Wales. On the other side of the mountain at the end of the Machno valley is the famous slate town of Blaenau Ffestiniog, and unsurprisingly there was also slate on the Penmachno side of the mountain. The population of Penmachno parish in the early 1800s, before the development of the quarries, was in the 600s, but when the slate quarries were at their peak the population was nearer 2,000. The quarries' expansion at the head of the valley resulted in the development of the village of Cwm Penmachno, about 3 miles from Penmachno itself. With the decline of the slate industry, and the last quarry closing in the early 1960s, the population of the parish is today again in the 600s.

Thomas' grandfather, William Williams, with his second wife Catherine

Thomas' grandfather, William Williams, was a quarryman. The photo shows William Williams with his second wife Catherine, whom he married following the death of his first wife with whom he had four sons.

William was one of five brothers. The eldest, John, was the first person to be killed in an accident in the Penmachno quarries in 1833. Another brother, Richard, was also a quarryman; he emigrated to Poultney in the 'Slate Valley' in Vermont, USA. A third brother, Bleddyn, left the quarries and worked as a gardener in Rhuddlan. A fourth brother, Ellis, stayed in Penmachno; he became a tailor, and there were many tailors amongst his descendants. Ellis was the grandfather of John Ellis Williams, the eminent Welsh dramatist and author, amongst whose many achievements was to write and produce the first Welsh-speaking film, *Y Chwarelwr* (*y*: the; *chwarelwr*: quarryman) in 1935. The family were devout Wesleyans. William and Ellis were both deacons for several decades at Bethania Chapel in Penmachno; Bleddyn was a deacon in Rhuddlan, and Richard in Poultney, Vermont.

William Williams had four sons: William (my great-grandfather), David, Owen and Evan. Whilst in his late teens, William decided to start using the middle name 'Pritchard'

William Pritchard Williams, Thomas' father, outside the back door of Talywaen, Penmachno

out of respect to his grandfather, William Pritchard, and also to distinguish himself from his father. William Pritchard Williams followed his father to work in the quarries and there is a record of him working at the Cwt y Bugail quarry, high on the mountainside above Cwm Penmachno, during the 1880s.

Before 1863 the

slate from the Penmachno quarries had to be taken down
the mountain to Cwm Penmachno and then taken by horse-
drawn trailers down the Machno and Conwy valleys to be
shipped from quays at Trefriw or Tal-y-Cafn. In 1863 the
Rhiw Bach Tramway was built by the partnership between
Owen Gethin Jones, his brother-in-law William Jones (one
of my great-great-great-grandfathers on my grandmother's
side) and his nephew Owen Jones (one of my great-great-
grandfathers). This tramway provided a link between the
Penmachno quarries at the top of the mountain and the
Blaenau Ffestiniog quarries on the other side. This allowed
transportation of the slate to the Ffestiniog railway and then
on to be shipped from Porthmadog. This was an enormous
boost to these quarries. Slate from the quarries at the
bottom of the mountain on the Penmachno side continued
to be sent to Tal-y-cafn and later to the railway station at
Betws-y-coed.

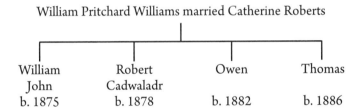

Thomas Williams, the fourth and youngest son of William
Pritchard Williams and wife Catherine, was born on 8
August 1886 at the family home, Talywaen, a terraced house
in the village of Penmachno. The shrewd grandfather,
William Williams, had taken a lease on Talywaen in 1866
and on 20 July 1867 William Williams purchased the house
with the aid of a mortgage from the North Denbighshire
Permanent Benefit Building Society, which was very active

in the developing industrial areas in northern Wales. On his remarriage following the death of his first wife, he sold the house to his son, William Pritchard Williams, on 21 February 1891.

Tom's elder brothers, William John and Robert Cadwaladr (my grandfather), followed their father to work in the quarry. This involved getting up very early on Monday morning, walking 3 miles from the village of Penmachno to Cwm Penmachno, and then walking up the mountainside to the quarry to start a hard day's work. They would then sleep at the barracks at the quarry during the week until Saturday morning, work the morning shift and then walk home on Saturday afternoon.

Following the collapse of a previous company, William Pritchard Williams was one of the leaders in 1893 in the establishment of a new company to operate the quarry, the Bugail Slate Quarry Company Limited. This was essentially a co-operative company with local people, mainly working at the quarry, purchasing £50 shares. William Pritchard Williams was one of the five directors, each of whom held three shares. His eldest son, William John was one of the initial shareholders and later Robert Cadwaladr also purchased a share from the widow of one of the original shareholders.

There is a family photo of the quarry men at Cwt y Bugail during the 1890s. William Pritchard, on the right at the end of the top row, is wearing a bowler hat. My grandfather, Robert Cadwaladr Williams, was born in 1878 and his appearance in the photograph (at the left of the third row) suggests that it was taken at the end of the 1890s. His elder brother, William John Williams, is seen further along the same row behind another man in a bowler hat.

Tom's mother Catherine died on 28 November 1896 when Tom was ten years old. Catherine would regularly

The quarrymen of Cwt y Bugail Quarry

pickle jars of red cabbage and one of the jars has survived. It's a splendid-looking bottle but the glass stopper has welded itself to the bottle, making it impossible to open and it is now on display as an object of interest in our house. I often wonder what the contents would taste like after over a hundred years!

Tom's mother Catherine

The two eldest sons were working at the quarry with their father at this time and living at the barracks during the week. William Pritchard Williams engaged a live-in housekeeper to care for the house and the two younger sons, Owen (who was then fourteen) and Tom (ten).

William Pritchard Williams wanted to ensure that his sons were well educated and there's a family photo showing the pupils at an evening class taken outside the then Penmachno National School. All four brothers are in this photo. In the back row, Robert Cadwaladr is on the far left, William John is the tall one fifth along and Owen is at the end on the right. Tom is the third from the right in second row. Robert and William John are of working age but Tom looks quite young, which probably dates the photo at around 1896–99. This would suggest that Robert Cadwaladr and William John would leave the quarry after work and make their way to Penmachno to attend evening class, and then make their way back to the quarry either that night or early the following morning. This was an enormous effort. I know that Robert purchased a bicycle in 1899 to help on his journeys. According to the receipt, it was a BSA bike bought from the Acme Wheeleries, Leeds, for £5-13-2, presumably purchased through a catalogue; the cost was quite high compared to the average wage of a quarryman.

Evening class outside Penmachno National School in the 1890s

Owen became an auctioneer's clerk in Llanrwst and was a lodger at Hyfrydle, Mount Pleasant, Llanrwst. He was in constant touch with the family and sent and received numerous postcards. At the beginning of the nineteenth century an address had to be put on one side of a postcard with the message being written on the other side, but in 1902 the rules changed so that messages could be written on the same side as the address. This led to the development of the picture postcard and the start of its golden age. During 1909, 800 million postcards were posted in Britain.

Tom's brother Owen

By 1904 Jennie Owen had become the housekeeper at Talywaen and many of the postcards were addressed to her. Fortunately she started keeping the postcards. Jennie subsequently married my grandfather, Robert Cadwaladr; my mother, Kate, was born in Talywaen in April 1909. Kate continued to collect the postcards and they have survived to become an invaluable resource for tracing family history.

Most of Owen's postcards were from fairly local locations, with many from Bodnant Gardens and Tal-y-cafn, one of which contains the message that he was at the Tal-y-cafn sale that day. This would suggest that there was an auction at Tal-y-cafn in those days. There was also an important quay a short distance down river from the Tal-y-cafn bridge which is where ships would be moored to take on slates from the Penmachno quarries.

An example of one of Owen's postcards shows a photo of

A steamer passes under the bridge at Tal-y-cafn

the pleasure steamer sailing up the Conwy river under the bridge at Tal-y-cafn. This steamer, known fondly in Welsh as '*stemar fach*' (*bach*: little), would travel regularly on the Conwy river between Conwy and Llanrwst until the 1930s. Unfortunately, Owen's health deteriorated in 1909, as can be seen from many of the messages on the postcards he received. He died unmarried on 1 November 1909, aged twenty-seven.

Tom is shown, aged fourteen, in the 1901 census as an apprentice tailor. William Williams' brother Ellis was a tailor, as were others in this branch of the family, and it's assumed that Tom served his apprenticeship with one of these.

In 1904 William Pritchard Williams and his son Robert Cadwaladr jointly purchased a 13-acre farm called Gwiga on the eastern side of the valley about 1½ miles from the village. They immediately rented out the land and started converting the traditional single-storey cottage into a two-storey house, a process which took four years to complete.

They did much of the work themselves, but the careful records and receipts kept showed that the conversion cost £132-16-6.

The quarry appeared to be going well until 1908, when there was a big rock fall and there were insufficient reserve funds to undertake the clearing work. Mortgages of £200 and £300 were taken out in July 1908 but these were not enough; a further mortgage of £1,700 was obtained from the Metropolitan Bank in April 1909. But the company went into voluntary liquidation in June. It transpires that William Pritchard Williams was the only director who signed for the £1,700 mortgage. He was found personally liable for the outstanding balance to the Metropolitan Bank and was declared bankrupt in September 1910, which caused considerable hardship for the family.

My grandparents, my mother (aged seven months) and William Pritchard Williams finally moved to live in Gwiga in November 1909. Gwiga was to be my grandparents' home until my grandfather's death in 1956. Gwiga was also where I have my earliest memories: I lived there with my grandparents during the 1940s whilst my father was in the forces.

2
1904-1914
Tom: Man about Town

There is an interesting postcard showing GwydIr Castle in Llanrwst sent 'with love' to Tom on 22 July 1904 from an unnamed girlfriend who clearly enjoyed his company and wants to know when he is coming to Llanrwst again. She wonders whether he arrived home before morning, which suggests that he was walking all the way from Llanrwst to Penmachno a distance of some 8 miles. The most interesting aspect is that she requests 'Bring that letter writing (*sic*) in French with you, for me to see it'. This suggests that Tom could read, write, and presumably speak French, which was quite remarkable for someone who was an apprentice tailor. This ability would turn out to be of enormous value to Tom in future years.

On completion of his apprenticeship Tom obtained his first job as a tailor in Oswestry. My grandfather had hardly been out of Penmachno and the neighbouring areas throughout his life but I remember my mother telling me that he'd gone on his bike to accompany Tom to Oswestry. It seems difficult to imagine them cycling along the A5 all that way with the bikes that were available at that time. However, I have the receipt to prove that my grandfather had a bike and Tom must also have had one.

A number of postcards between November 1904 and December 1905 confirm that he was working in Oswestry but there's no clue as to the name of his employer. A card showing Oswestry School, dated January 1906, indicates that he was looking for a change. He writes in Welsh to say that he has changed lodgings and that he has placed an

Postcard of GwydIr Castle, and the message on the back from an unknown girlfriend of Tom's

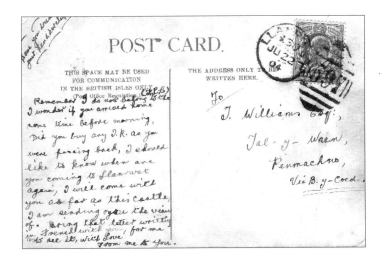

Postcard from Oswestry, with message on the back from Tom to his father, who was living, during the week, at the Bugail Slate Quarry

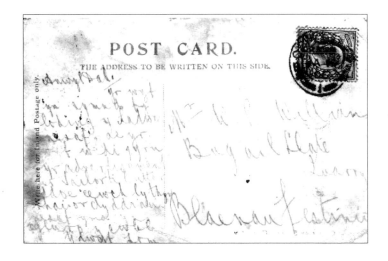

advertisement in the trade journal, the *Tailor and Cutter*. This probably meant that he'd posted an advert to say that he was looking for a new position. This card is addressed to his father at the Bugail Slate Quarry. His father would have been staying at the barracks at the quarry during the week and this would have been the best address to which to send any correspondence. Note that whilst the quarry was in the parish of Penmachno, the address is Blaenau Ffestiniog as mail, along with all

Shop of T. S. Atkins, Tailor, in Barnoldswick, Lancs, where Tom worked for a time in 1906

supplies, would have been delivered to the quarry through Blaenau Ffestiniog via the Rhiw Bach Tramway.

Shortly after this card was sent Tom moved to Barnoldswick in Lancashire, near the Yorkshire border, from where he sent postcards dated between February and August 1906. He worked with T. S. Atkinson, Ladies and Gents' Tailors, which looks from the postcard to be a rather modest shop. From other cards it looks as if there were some attractive places in and around Barnoldswick. However, cards during August 1906 suggest that he was out of work and looking for another job.

From September 1906 the postcards started coming from Colwyn Bay where he had found employment with H. R. Davies, Ladies and Gentlemen's Tailor, of Holborn House, 67 Abergele Road, Colwyn Bay. Apart from his time in the war he spent the rest of his working life in this

The staff of H. R. Davies' tailoring business in Colwyn Bay; Tom is standing behind the girl with the white blouse

business in Colwyn Bay. The photo shows the staff of H. R. Davies taken during the period 1907–1915. Tom is seen standing behind the girl in the white blouse.

The address on the first card from Colwyn Bay shows that he was living in Fern Royd, Erskin Road, but by the 1911 census Tom was living as a lodger in Gwelfor, 2 Grove Road, Colwyn Bay, very convenient for working in the shop. The householder, Hugh Roberts, was described as working as a pawnbroker.

There are numerous postcards from Tom to his family in Penmachno during his period in Colwyn Bay. One shows the

The entrance to Colwyn Bay pier, around 1908

Pier Entrance, and was sent on 20 July 1908 to Jennie Owen, my grandmother before she married. The pier looks absolutely splendid and they are advertising the 'Riviere's Grand Orchestra' and, in addition to the notice board, the name is up in large letters on the building. Jules Riviere was a French musician who became musical director at the Llandudno Pier Pavilion in 1887 and established a 42-piece orchestra. When the Colwyn Bay Pier Pavilion opened he and his orchestra moved there. Riviere died in 1900 but clearly his orchestra carried on.

A postcard sent on 24 August 1908, again to my grandmother, shows St Paul's Cathedral. This is the first of a number of postcards that show that Tom was taking regular holidays in London during the summers. Not many young men would have been taking holidays like this in those days, but Tom must have been saving his money for these trips so as to expand his experiences.

On 15 October 1908 Tom sent a card to his brother Owen at the family home saying that he was pleased to hear that he was better and would be coming to see him on Saturday. This is one of numerous cards from people with comments

Pwllycrochan Hotel, Colwyn Bay, posted 1908

regarding Owen's health during 1908–9. The card shows the Pwllycrochan Hotel which looks a splendid building. It was the sale of the Pwllycrochan Estate that kick-started the development of Colwyn Bay as a seaside resort. Pwllycrochan Hall was the heart of the estate and was remodelled as a hotel. It flourished as a hotel into the beginning of the last century and in 1937 hosted the Grand Coronation Ball. During the Second World War it was requisitioned by the government and it wasn't until 1948 that it reopened as a hotel, with seventy-five bedrooms. Business wasn't so good after the war and the hotel closed in 1952. It was sold to Rydal School, who moved their Preparatory School there in 1953.

On 6 October 1909 Tom was in Liverpool for the day, and sent a card to my grandmother reporting that the weather was good. The photo is interesting in that it shows a view of the landing stage, which is very different from the view that is seen today with the wonderful Liver, Cunard and the Liverpool Dock Board Buildings giving a magnificent waterfront scene. This card shows only the splendid Liverpool Dock Board

Liverpool waterfront, 1909, with Liverpool Dock Board buildings; this was prior to the Liver Building (1911) and the Cunard Building (1916)

Buildings, which were completed in 1907. The other two iconic Liverpool Pier Head buildings had not been built at that time: the Liver Building was started in 1908 and completed in 1911 and the Cunard Building was built between 1913 and 1916. It would appear that the Liverpool landing stage area wasn't at all spectacular before these fine buildings were built.

Tom sent a card to his father dated 22 November 1909. An interesting aspect of this card is that it is the first one addressed to Gwiga rather than Talywaen. Tom says that he is pleased to hear that the family had moved to Gwiga and that they liked the place and that he would be coming to see them in their new home on Saturday. There is an additional note on the top asking 'how is Kate?', who was about seven months old at this time. It was from this card that I was able to establish the date when the family moved to Gwiga.

Tom sent a card from Dublin showing the O'Connell Bridge with the caption 'Remarkable for its width'. This is dated 26 December 1909, so he must have taken a few days holiday over Christmas. He wrote that he had been very ill on the ferry crossing!

O'Connell Bridge in Dublin, 1909

*Tom and friends, Colwyn Bay, before the start of the War
(above, Tom second from right; below, Tom on right)*

Two photos were taken during his time in Colwyn Bay before the war. The first shows five young men sitting outside a tent having tea. They are all formally dressed with stiff collars, white shirts and waistcoats – remarkably formally dressed for a group of campers! They have a table with a cloth and a jam jar with flowers on the table. They have china cups and saucers and a china tea pot. Tom is the second from the right.

Another photo shows four young men and a dog in a posed photo that looks as if it has been taken in a photographer's studio. Tom, sitting on the right, and his friends certainly look as if they enjoyed dressing up smartly. These photos remind me of P. G. Wodehouse's 'young men about town'. Many of P. G. Wodehouse's books were written about this period and these photos conjure up images of the Wodehouse characters.

There are postcards from London showing that he was there on holiday during August 1911, 1912 and 1913 and another from Dublin in 1910. There are also numerous postcards from other places such as Chester, Liverpool, New Brighton etc. where he had been on day visits. The image that we get about Tom's life in Colwyn Bay before the war is that he was a young man who was socialising and enjoying himself and taking regular holidays in London during the summer, with occasional holidays elsewhere, as well as frequent day trips.

The last photo shows that Tom was a good-looking young man.

Tom as a young man

3
1914-1915
Recruiting

War was declared on 4 August 1914. It affected everyone in the country. Tom enlisted in November 1915 (see Chapters 4–9). His brother Robert Cadwaladr, my grandfather, was also called up for military service in November 1916 but he decided to go to a Tribunal to ask to be excused military service. By this time my grandfather had left the quarry and was working as a postman in addition to running a small farm. *The Welsh Coast Pioneer*, 14 December 1916, carried the following report regarding a Tribunal:

> **A Valley of Eldorado**
> Robert C Williams, Gwiga Farm, Penmachno who applied said that he kept 200 fowls and sent 400 to 500 eggs a week to Llanrwst market. The Chairman dryly remarked that he had discovered a fortune. The applicant, who complained of ill health, consented to undergo medical examination and the case was deferred pending the medical report.

Whilst the Tribunal Chairman was clearly sceptical about the number of eggs sold, my grandparents certainly did sell eggs. I show a postcard sent from the Waterloo Hotel, Betws-y-coed, in August 1914 where the message is, 'We can manage without eggs until the 21st as we are not so busy'. The Waterloo Hotel was the largest hotel in Betws-y-coed and the magnificent building seen in the photo was pulled down about 1970, following which the present day Waterloo Hotel was built.

A second postcard dated 1 November 1914 from the Waterloo Hotel shows a very different situation with the

Waterloo Hotel, Betws-y-coed; postcard sent in August 1914

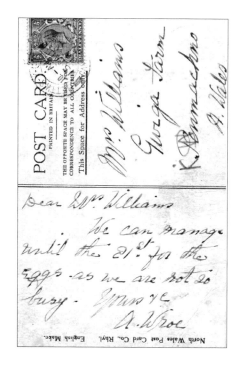

Happy Valley, Llandudno, summer 1914 – a few weeks from the start of the War

message, 'Will you kindly call with eggs as soon as possible and as many as you can'!

Another example is a postcard showing a very busy Happy Valley in Llandudno in 1914 with many people enjoying the open-air show and an excellent view of the pier. The message reads, 'Will you send 2 or 3 pounds of butter and 2/- of eggs on Friday with Mrs Davies. W. G. Atkinson.' Uncle Tom had been a tailor with T. S. Atkinson in Barnoldswick, Lancashire, in 1906 and I've often wondered whether there was a connection between these Atkinsons.

Geirionydd Tribunal: Postman exempted

Robert C Williams, Gwiga Farm, Penmachno whose appeal at the previous court was adjourned to enable the applicant to appear before a medical board at Wrexham, now produced a certificate classifying him as Cii. Conditional exemption granted, subject to the applicant resigning as a postman within seven days and restricting his energies to farm work.

North Wales Weekly News, 11 January 1917

Whilst my grandfather had been excused military duty, he had been punished by losing his job as a postman. By the time I first knew him in the early 1940s he was once again working as a postman in addition to running the small farm with four cows. I remember accompanying my grandmother taking butter and eggs to Llanrwst on market days on Tuesdays and the monthly fair on a Wednesday. At that time, however, during WW2 all farm produce had to be taken to the Packing Station in the Market Hall and sold to the government (other than that which was sold on the Black Market, of course, but that's another story!).

There were campaigns to gather support for the war and amongst them was the postcard that was circulating in Wales to get people to show their support for the war. The card shown was sent on 16 September 1916, to 'Wm Wms Bach' (William Pritchard Williams, Tom's father) by '*Yr Awdur*' (*awdur*: author). '*Yr Awdur*' was presumably the designer and publisher of the card, John Robert Gethin Jones. He was a son of Owen Gethin Jones, the civil engineering contractor, bard and local historian, whose business partner was Owen Jones, one of my great-great-grandfathers on my grandmother' side. Gwiga was the neighbouring farm to Tyddyn Cethin, where John Robert had spent his childhood. John Robert would have known William Pritchard Williams well.

John Robert was a successful engineer and accomplished metrologist (the science of weights and measures), and the card is very detailed and well worth examining with a magnifying glass. This is a chain postcard with the following instructions at the bottom:

TO WIN THE WAR, let us follow the example of the Modern David in a determined Push, and go out in earnest – Fight, Work and Economise – we can all do

Postcard intended to engender financial support for the War

something. The service that I'm doing is – see the link between yours and LLOYD-GEORGE, – You know well that VICTORY depends on our UNITED PUSH. So please fill up the LINK received, retain it as a keepsake. Send another to your friend until the CHAIN will be long enough to surround the ENEMY. Beware of a gap.

The card has six hearts connecting the Kingdom of Heaven; David (slayer of Goliath); Saint David from the sixth century and 'the Push and Go David', David Lloyd George, from the twentieth century. The fifth heart is from 'The Sender' with the date 16 September 1916 with a promise written to 'pay' and from this one can assume that John Robert was making a financial contribution to the war. The final heart is for the recipient to complete and it is seen that William Pritchard did not follow the instruction to sign this section!

The card has strong imagery linked with the Welsh National Eisteddfod such as 'Awake it is day' at the top which is repeated in Welsh at the bottom, *'Deffro mae'n ddydd'*, which is one of the slogans of Iolo Morganwg, the founder of the modern National Eisteddfod. *'Y gwir yn erbyn y byd'*, ('The truth against the world' in English) under the hearts is the slogan of the Eisteddfod. Underneath this is the three strokes symbol of the Bardic Circle.

The slogan 'Ideal of the Little Nation' conjures up the link with Belgium which was emphasised, by David Lloyd George and others, as a small nation overrun by the Germans. The music in the centre is the opening bars of the Welsh National anthem, 'Land of my fathers'.

Radiating out of 'The Day' in the centre are three slogans 'Liberty, the best power – knowledge'; 'Justice, the best medium – light' and 'Fraternity, the best weapon – education'.

The pillars on either side of the map of Wales show, in Welsh on one side and English on the other, 'The Welsh Nation' with the date 1282, the conquest by Edward I; the date 1911, the investiture of Edward (later Edward VIII) as Prince of Wales at Caernarfon Castle and 1914, the outbreak of the war.

On the leaves growing out of the columns are the slogans in Welsh and English, 'Loyalty, Service'; 'Grief, Sacrifice'; 'Pay, compromise, work, fight'; 'Kingdom of Heaven, Liberty, Peace, Victory'; 'Patience, Endurance'; 'Devotion, Courage'; 'Better Death than Shame' and 'Duty'. There are some remarkable connections here and on the sword is the remarkable slogan 'Kill for good'!

The card conjures up Welsh nationalistic feelings, but at the top are the Union flag on one side and the Prince of Wales' feathers on the other, and the slogan 'Victory depends on our United Push' and in the centre, the slogan 'Tho. language differ, Patriotism unites'. The card utilises Welsh nationalist feelings, but implies that only through unity will victory be achieved.

This really is a fascinating card. It would be interesting to know how many copies of this card have survived.

Another example of the influence of the war on everyday life is the school certificate my mother received at the end of the summer term in 1916. I haven't got an example of a pre-war school certificate but I'm sure that it wouldn't have had all the royal symbolism! It has been produced by the well-known educational supplier E. J. Arnold and presumably offered to all counties, with each county inserting its own wording in the centre. The Caernarvonshire wording is all in Welsh with my mother's name, together with the name of the school, written in. The Chairman of the Education Committee was William George, brother of David Lloyd George.

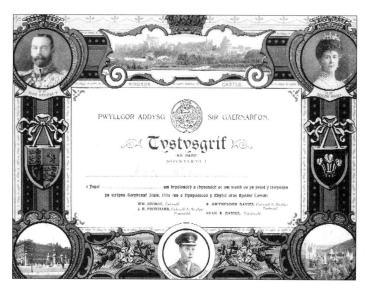

Tom's niece Kate's school certificate, 1916, with much royalist symbolism

4
1915-1916
The Liverpool Scottish Battalion

On 21 November 1915 Tom enlisted in Colwyn Bay with The King's Liverpool Regiment, 10th Battalion, known as the Liverpool Scottish. The Battalion conducted recruitment campaigns in the towns along the North Wales coast. Tom might have joined this battalion because some of his friends had done so or perhaps he was attracted by the uniform. In his photograph he certainly looks smart in his kilt.

Tom in the uniform of the Liverpool Scottish Battalion

We in Wales – particularly in the north of the country – are very much aware of the strong Welsh elements in Liverpool, which was at one time considered by many to be the 'capital of North Wales'. There were also strong Irish and Scottish elements in Liverpool. As a result of events in France during 1859 there were movements throughout Britain to form Volunteer Units to support the regular army and these laid the foundation of the subsequent establishment in 1909 of the Territorial Army. In Liverpool the Scots got together and formed the Liverpool Scottish Rifles in January 1860.

There were further developments with the Scottish Volunteers during the rest of the century but it was the Boer

War which saw the establishment of the 'Scottish Battalion' in 1900 which became the 8th Volunteer Battalion of The King's (Liverpool) Regiment. Despite initial War Office instructions that the dress should be tartan trews, it was agreed in April 1901 that the official dress should be Highland dress, and that the kilt should be worn. A small group of one officer and twenty-two other ranks from this Volunteer Battalion served in South Africa in 1902.

In March 1908, The Territorial and Reserve Forces Act 1907 was implemented to disband the Volunteer Force and

Tom (seated, left) in training

establish the more structured Territorial Force. The 8th (Scottish) Volunteer Battalion was disbanded and the 10th (Scottish) Battalion, The King's (Liverpool) Regiment was formed and Tom joined this Battalion in November 1915.

The photo shows ten soldiers taken during the initial training period, most of whom are wearing the apron over the kilt. Tom is sitting at the left as you look at the photo and as he is not wearing the apron his sporran can be seen clearly.

He was Pte No. 5707/356976 and was posted to C

Tom writes to Kate from Southport to say he is there for firing practice

Tom's battalion on the beach at Blackpool, awaiting embarkation

Company at Weeton Camp near Blackpool for his initial training. On 15 March 1916 he sent a card to my mother from 30 Lytham Rd, Marsh Side, Southport, saying that he was there for two weeks for firing practice.

The above photo is of the Battalion on the beach at

Blackpool before embarkation. This card, dated 9 April 1916 and postmarked Birmingham, was sent to his father (William P. Williams of Gwiga, Penmachno) and on the back is written in Welsh, 'Off to France tomorrow. See me behind the dot. Will write soon'. Tom's army records show that he did embark for France on 10 April 1916.

Finding Tom's Army Records
Whilst researching family history at the National Archives at Kew I investigated whether Tom's army records could be found. Arround 70 per cent of all the WW1 records had been destroyed as the building where they were being kept had been bombed during WW2. I therefore had a 30 per cent chance of finding Tom's records. The records were kept on microfilm. 'Thomas Williams' is a common name and I found that there were eight reels containing records for soldiers named Thomas Williams. I started on the first reel and found that many of the records that had survived were damaged and not very easy to read and it didn't help that I didn't, at that time, know his address when he enlisted. It was a slow difficult task – but imagine my joy when I eventually found Tom's records towards the end of seventh reel! By today these records are available on websites such as Ancestry and searches are much easier. The quality of the records on the website is also better than the photocopies I obtained from the microfilm.

After finding these records in Kew I decided to seek further information about Tom's life in the army and discovered that there was a Liverpool Scottish Museum in Liverpool. I made contact and visited the Museum and found the archivist, Dennis Reeves, to be extremely helpful. The museum has since had to close because the lease came to an end, but the archives continue to be kept and arrangements to visit can be made. Dennis and the

Honorary Secretary, Major Ian Riley, have been an enormous help to me in providing more information about Tom's records and providing background information on the Liverpool Scottish.

Lieutenant Noel Godfrey Chavasse

Amongst the officers of the Liverpool Scottish there were many highly intelligent men. I'll mention two as their names will feature in some of the following chapters. The medical officer was Lieutenant Noel Godfrey Chavasse, son of the Rev. Francis Chavasse, then Bishop of Liverpool and founder of St. Peter's College, Oxford. He graduated from Oxford with first class honours and then went on to study medicine in Liverpool under the prominent Welsh orthopaedic surgeon, Sir Robert Jones, and he himself became a prominent orthopaedic surgeon. He qualified as a doctor in July 1912 and obtained his first placement at the Royal Southern Hospital in Liverpool and later became house surgeon to Sir Robert Jones, whose name lives on today in the name of The Robert Jones and Agnes Hunt Orthopedic Hospital, Gobowen, near Oswestry.

In early 1913 he was accepted by the Royal Army Medical Corps and commissioned a Lieutenant on 2 June and was attached to the Liverpool Scottish. He now had to attend both his hospital and his military duties. At the commencement of the war he gave up his civilian hospital employment and became the medical officer with the Liverpool Scottish.

Company Quartermaster Sergeant Robert Andrew Scott Macfie

Robert Andrew Scott Macfie was a highly intelligent graduate educated at Cambridge, Edinburgh and Göttingen Universities before joining the sugar refining business which his family had owned and operated in Liverpool since 1788. His interests included Gypsy Studies and the Romani way of life and he became a leading authority on Roma/Gypsies and their language, recording vast quantities of dialect, folk-tales and songs from various bands of Roma/Gypsies in Britain. He revived the Gypsy Lore Society in 1907 and contributed research work to the Journal of the Gypsy Lore Society. He had previously served with the old Volunteer battalion and at the beginning of the war he rejoined the Liverpool Scottish as the Company Quartermaster Sergeant. He was the only Quartermaster Sergeant in the British Army, at that time at least, to compile and publish a practical and comprehensive Army Cookery Book, 'Things that Every Good Cook Should Know'. It contained nearly seventy recipes and information on cleanliness, economy and cookhouse routine.

An outline of the Liverpool Scottish activities August 1914 – April 1916

At the start of the war the Liverpool Scottish were based in Edinburgh and were sent to Tunbridge Wells for further training in October 1914. They were amongst the first Territorial Infantry battalions to be selected for overseas duty and arrived in France on 3 November 1914. They settled in Blendecques and were in reserve for the First Battle of Ypres but were not called upon. Major J. R. Davidson, an engineer by profession, became the Commanding Officer. They were sent to the lines at Kemmel, south-west of Ypres in Belgium, on 27 November 1914.

They spent the winter getting used to the horrific conditions of trench warfare but were fortunate to be out of the line on Christmas Day 1914. The Christmas mail was colossal with more than 250 sacks received; an indication of the support from family and public back home. There was an active Ladies' Committee which worked at knitting and collecting socks, caps, cardigans etc building up stocks to be sent to France as required. There were also generous contributions to enable additional rations to be sent out regularly. The Medical Officer, Lieutenant Chavasse, regularly received difficult-to-obtain drugs and medicines from friends in Liverpool and he once obtained a drug unobtainable in Britain from a friend in the USA.

They experienced action on the front line during early 1915 but had their first experience of major action in June 1915 when they were part of an attack to capture three lines of enemy trenches near the village of Hooge east of Ypres. The Liverpool Scottish certainly distinguished themselves in this battle. They succeeded in their objectives and held the captured ground for some time until ordered to withdraw because their flanks were exposed.

It was a horrific battle on 16 June and a costly action for the Liverpool Scottish. Of the twenty-three officers and 519 men who went into action only two officers and 140 men came out unscathed. On 16 June 1915, 150 of all ranks were killed in action and many died of wounds later. Some were captured and many found their way back wounded and were evacuated to the UK for hospital treatment. The future of such a small battalion was in doubt but they were reinforced by newly-trained recruits from Britain and were able to continue in action. The actions of the stretcher-bearers received special mention. They did splendid work during the action and stayed behind after the Battalion was relieved and worked through the night of the 16th and the following night until they were satisfied that every wounded man had been brought in. An inspiring example was set by the Medical Officer, Lieutenant Chavasse, who personally continually searched the ground between the lines. He was awarded the Military Cross for his outstanding work, and one of the stretcher-bearers, Pte F. F. Bell, was awarded the Distinguished Conduct Medal.

Other men were also decorated for their outstanding contribution at Hooge. Three men who received the DCM had been recommended by the Commanding Officers of other units and a further ten men were awarded the Military Cross for conspicuous gallantry. The Battalion was praised by the senior officers and the following impartial comment was made by a Gordon Highlander:

> My division has just been over the top at Hooge. We were in the reserve behind and I saw the finest sight I'll ever see. I saw the Liverpool Scottish make their attack and they went over as if they were on parade.

The Liverpool Scottish remained in the Ypres area serving in various trenches during the remainder of 1915. In January 1916 the Liverpool Scottish became part of the 166th Brigade, 55th (West Lancashire) Division and, following a new draft of recruits, at the end of January consisted of twenty-two officers and 393 men. By February 1916 they were moved to the Rivière Sector some six miles south of Arras in France where they served for a number of months. The country around Rivière was rolling country of low hills and wide valleys, practically undamaged and still under cultivation which was a complete contrast with the Ypres area.

5
1916
France

Tom and his draft of new recruits arrived in France on 11 April 1916 and this was one of six drafts of 700 new recruits which raised the strength of the Liverpool Scottish to 1,000 by July. Rivière district, south of Arras, where the Liverpool Scottish was now based, was made up of three villages, Grosville, Bellacourt and Bretencourt. The first two had hardly been subjected to shelling and most of the civilian population was still present. Bretencourt, however, being more exposed, had suffered greatly and most of the inhabitants had fled.

As the Battalion had been in the Rivière area for some time they had established, under the leadership of Medical Officer Lieutenant Chavasse, some good facilities such as a bath-house in the yard of a brewery in Bellacourt where men were able to bathe. A laundry was established, for socks being collected from each man on the lines in the mornings and returned the following morning in exchange for a dirty pair. This facility was extended later to include the men's towels and finally their kilts. However, the men had to take responsibility for drying and ironing their own kilts as the laundry could not cope with this activity. It's difficult to understand how the men coped with this task. They also established a canteen with a Corporal W Forbes touring the trenches in the mornings taking the men's orders and delivering it in the afternoons. These were amazing facilities at this time and it was said that at no time during the war was the Battalion more efficient than at the time it left Rivière.

This is where Tom was stationed when he sent the first communication from France in my possession which was the

Field Service postcard sent from France, June 1916, with (on back) standard phrases, giving no specific information

standard Field Service Card dated 12 June 1916 addressed to my mother, aged seven. The back of the card shows that the sender is not allowed to write anything and only has a choice of a number of standard phrases. Tom has written, 'I am quite well and am going on well. Letter follows at first opportunity.' I can only imagine how a family would feel if they had received a similar card, but saying 'I have been admitted to hospital wounded. Letter follows at first opportunity,' and then having to wait until

the letter arrived with the details.

The next postcard is an example of the embroidered silk cards known as 'WW1 Silks'. They were mostly produced by French and Belgian women refugees who worked in their homes and refugee camps, and then sent the finished strips to factories for cutting and mounting on postcards. They were wildly popular with British

Silk cards were produced by French and Belgian women refugees. This one was sent by Tom from Bellacourt, Arras

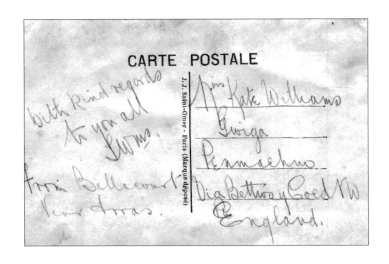

and American servicemen on duty in France. There is no stamp on this and it was clearly sent in an envelope with a letter but it must have been sent during this period as Tom has added to it later in pencil, 'Sent from Bellacourt near Arras'.

The Battle of the Somme officially started on 1 July 1916. On 12 July the Liverpool Scottish took over trenches at Agny for a few days. They were then moved a couple of times before ending up further south near Méricourt, and finally to what was known as the Sand Pit area about 2 miles south-east of the town of Albert by 27 July.

On 29 July 1916 Tom sent his first postcard from France addressed to my mother which shows a bombed church showing the date of 20 June 1915 which was presumably when the church was bombed. All subsequent cards were addressed to my mother and it's difficult to imagine a child aged between seven and nine during 1916 to 1918 receiving postcards with such horrific photos. It is seen that the sensor has blacked out the location name on the card. On the back

Card showing bombed church, dated June 1915 –
the censor has crossed out the location

Tom has written, 'Just a card for your collection. Going on alright. Letter to follow shortly. Put Y Co. on the letters please. Yours, Tom Wms'.

On 30 July they moved to Mansel Copse, half a mile south of Mametz where there had been fierce fighting in Mametz Wood during July resulting in huge losses by the Welsh Regiment. A magnificent large painting of the Battle of Mametz Wood by Christopher Williams can be seen in the Royal Welsh Fusiliers Museum in Caernarfon. Here the Liverpool Scottish was subjected to enemy bombing and had a very busy six days digging communications and cable trenches.

The second card from France, dated 3 August 1916 shows a battle scene from 1914. It was written on 1 August and it has the stamp and signature of the censor on it. On the back Tom says that he is 'alright' and that the weather is 'frightfully hot'. He thanks the family for offering to send food and says he would like some cake. However, I wonder what sort of state a cake would be in after being sent all that way!

Battle of Guillemont

On 6 August the Liverpool Scottish went back to camp with orders to be ready for an attack on the village of Guillemont. On the 7th the bombardment started and on 8 August they went into action and there followed a horrific battle. The Battalion went into action with twenty officers and about 600 other ranks. The remainder of the Battalion were being deliberately kept back to ensure a core remained in the event of heavy losses. At the end of the battle they had lost five officers killed, five missing and seven wounded. In other ranks sixty-nine had been killed, twenty-seven missing and 167 wounded. Afterwards it was found that nearly all the missing officers and men had been killed.

During the battle there were large numbers of wounded men lying out in no-man's-land and a number of men again distinguished themselves by crawling out to dress wounds, giving water and carrying them to safety. Amongst these was the Medical Officer, Captain Noel Chavasse, who was awarded the Victoria Cross for his outstanding bravery in risking his own life. The official citation is as follows:

> During the attack on Guillemont, on August 9th, this officer continued to tend the wounded in the open all day under heavy fire, frequently exposing himself to view of the enemy. He organised parties to get the wounded away most successfully. That night he spent four hours searching the ground in front of the enemy's lines for wounded laying-out. On the following day he proceeded with one stretcher-bearer to the advanced trenches and carried an urgent case for 500 yards under a very heavy shell fire. During this performance he was wounded in the side by a shell splinter. The same night he took up a party of 20 volunteers, and succeeded in recovering three more of the wounded from a shell-hole 25 yards from the German trench, buried the bodies of two officers, and collected a number of identity-discs, although fired on by bombs and machine-guns. Altogether this officer was the means of saving the lives of 20 seriously wounded men under the most trying circumstances, besides the ordinary cases which passed through his hands. At the time, when all the officers were shot down, he helped to rally the firing-line.

The battalion came out of the lines on 14 August and marched back to billets. Following this battle five men received the Distinguished Conduct Medal; two received the Military Cross and a further eight Military Medals were awarded. This was an unusually large allocation of decorations to a battalion which had taken part in what was unfortunately an unsuccessful attack. When things had gone well rewards were, as a rule, distributed on a fairly lavish scale, but they were very hard to come by after a failure, so it is an indication of how well the Liverpool Scottish had performed. Tom was, of course, in the middle of this, his first experience of a major battle.

On 16 August 1916 they were inspected by Major-General Jeudwine, Commander of the 55th West Lancashire Division, who thanked them and praised them for their activities at Guillemont. His address included the following:

> I saw you in the attack on 16 June 1915 (the Battle of Hooge). I know what the Battalion has done, what it can do and what it will do; I know what sort of men it is made up of. I remember the dash with which you went and the stubbornness with which you stuck there, and whenever you are asked to do anything of the sort again you will do it with all your old dash. The determination and effort, not only once but twice, to get over shows that the Battalion is as great a battalion to overcome difficulties as it was before, and as it always will be.

On 17 August Tom send this remarkable card showing the efforts being made to encourage the families to write to the soldiers. It shows sad service men who have not received any mail and happy men who have received some mail – 'see how sad we are' and 'see how gay we are when the sergeant gives us our letters'. There is also an exhortation to all families to address their mail correctly. (This card was produced in the days when the word 'gay' was used in the sense of 'happy'.)

Tom acknowledges the receipt of a letter and parcel and says that 'We are going on rest for a short time after our

See how gay we are when the sargent gives us our letters.

Quick, Give me some news from you.

See how sad we are when we don't have any mail.

For ... sake please write carefully the adress to facilitate ... job ... of our P. O. Sargent

Tom sends Kate a card produced to encourage families to write to soldiers to keep up their morale

great charge. Still feeling in the pink'. This sums up Tom's optimistic reaction following the horrific battle and there is more on his experiences at Guillemont in Chapter 6. The phrase 'in the pink' was used frequently in my childhood. It had largely gone out of use before the end of the twentieth century, but it was clearly well used during the Great War period as it comes up frequently.

There is a note at the top saying 'Trusting that Jennie (my grandmother) and Katie will enjoy their holiday. Give my kind regards to her mother (my great grandmother)'. Presumably my grandmother was taking a rare holiday by going to stay with her mother, who was working in Southport during this period.

There is another note written in pencil in Welsh later which says 'I wrote this before I hurt my foot'. His records show that he injured his ankle on 18 August and was sent to a field hospital and subsequently sent home and arrived in the UK on 22 August. It's not clear how he sustained this

Photograph of Kate, to whom Tom's cards and messages were addressed

injury but he was not on the battlefield at this time. Tom was now in Britain and away from the horrors of war, much to the relief of his family.

The Liverpool Scottish left the battlefield on 19 August by train to Martainville and then marched to Valines, west of Abbeyfield some 10 miles from the coast. They expected a few weeks' rest here but on 28 August they were on the way back to the lines and on 30 August arrived at Méricourt (to the north of Arras) and were soon back in action.

6
1916-1917
Hospital

On his return, Tom was sent to hospital at the Auxillary Millitary Institute, Church Street, Ashton-under Lyne, from where he started communicating with family and friends and he kept a couple of post cards.

There was an interesting report in the *Welsh Coast Pioneer* on 14 September 1916 which reports on a letter that Tom had sent to his boss H. R. Davies, the tailor in Colwyn Bay. The report is reproduced below but the reporter has made the unfortunate error of using Newcastle-on-Tyne instead of Ashton-under-Lyne! However the report does refer to the 'Manchester people'.

Private Tom Williams, Colwyn Bay

Private Tom Williams, Liverpool Scottish, well known as an assistant to Mr H R Davies, tailor, Abergele Road, Colwyn Bay, is in hospital at Newcastle-on-Tyne, suffering from an injured ankle. His experience of hospital life in France is fairly extensive, as he has been a patient in three of them, and he says of an Australian hospital that it is 'first class'. The fighting at Guillemont in which he took part, he says, was 'like hell' and he marvels at his own escape with his life. He is doing well at Newcastle. 'It is heaven to be here,' he writes. He has a great deal to say about the kindness shown by Manchester people to wounded soldiers arriving there. 'We had a great reception,' he says, 'the people cheered us and threw cigs and flowers into our cars. I shall never forget it'.

His references to the hospitals in France before he was evacuated home are interesting and his reference to the battle at Guillemont makes me really wish my grandmother had kept Tom's letters to his family. The reception he and his colleagues received are an indication of how highly people at home regarded those who were serving in the war. The first sentence is interesting as it describes Tom as 'well known as an assistant to Mr H R Davies, tailor' which confirms that Tom was a well-liked person.

The next card from Stockport, dated 24 September, is from a friend named Bob, who says that he has also been sent home and is in hospital in nearby Stockport. He says that he is suffering from 'heart and nerves' which I assume could mean the 'shell-shock' which so many men suffered in WW1. He asks, 'how do you think that you'll like Blighty?'!

There are two photos of patients taken outside the hospital, which appears to be a large building. The first is a group of twenty-four; Tom is the third from the left sitting on the ground with his leg bandaged and stretched out. It looks as if he has a brace on the leg. He is wearing his 'hospital blues', which is what the Liverpool Scottish wore in hospitals.

There are men in civilian suits in the second photo and also some children. Tom is the fourth from the right in the second row behind those on the ground. The fact that he is able to sit in a chair suggests that this is the latter of the two photos.

The next card from the hospital, written in Welsh, is dated 30 September. He gives thanks for a letter and is pleased that they've completed the harvest and pleased that it's been a good one. He wishes he could come to visit. He is getting on well and thinks he'll be in hospital, which is an excellent place where he gets everything he needs, for another week or so.

A card date September 1916 from Tom's friend Bob, who says he is in hospital in Stockport 'suffering from heart and nerves'

Tom in hospital in Ashton-under-Lyne. In the top photograph Tom is third from left in the front row; in the lower photo he is fourth from right in the second row

The photo shown on the back cover is dated 26 October and gives an address of Hut 16, H Coy., Burry Old Road Camp, Heaton Park, Manchester. The message in Welsh is 'Here as a convalescent. Very good place. Letter soon.' Interestingly, he's used a postcard that he must have purchased whilst in France. It shows wounded soldiers and one soldier being carried on a stretcher. The caption is

'Somme push. Huns carry in wounded Frenchmen.' This would suggest that German prisoners were being used to carry the wounded.

Tom was in the 1st Battalion of the Liverpool Scottish and there was also a 2nd Battalion engaged in military activities in France. In May 1915 a 3rd Battalion was formed as a draft-finding unit for the 1st and 2nd Battalions to prepare them for action. They were initially based in Blackpool but in May/June 1916 the West Lancashire Division moved to Park Hall Camp between Gobowen and Oswestry in Shropshire and this is where the battalion stayed for the remainder of the war.

When he was considered to be fit, Tom was sent to the Park Hall Camp where he was based until he was again sent to France on 10 June 1917.

In the meantime, back in France, the Liverpool Scottish saw action on the lines during September, and in October 1916 they were moved north ending up in the line in the Wieltje sector north-east of Ypres. In November they took part in a raid on what was known as 'Kaiser Bill'. During the early part of 1917 they were still involved in active service on the lines with periodic rest periods. On 14 June, by which time Tom had probably joined the rest of the battalion, they were relieved from front line duty and by 20 June 1917 had moved to the village of Zadausques, some 5 miles west of St. Omer. Tom was now back with the Battalion in France ready to participate once more in the war.

7

1917

Back in France

On 20 June the Battalion arrived in Zadausques, some 5 miles west of St Omer, and on 21 June Tom sent home the Joan of Arc postcard and on the back he's written, 'We are still at base camp having a fairly easy time, weather very hot, will write to you again when we are more settled down.' This, unfortunately, is the only postcard that I have from this period.

As it was thought that the

Postcard portraying Joan of Arc, and giving news of very hot weather in France; June 1917

Battalion would be in Zadausques for some time the Company Quartermaster Sargent, Scott McFie, suggested that it might be worthwhile to open a Beer Garden which could be the centre of recreational activities for the Battalion.

The suggestion was immediately adopted and a committee was formed. Macfie went to St. Omer to arrange for the printing of posters and to buy a piano. After considerable difficulty he eventually managed to buy a second-hand piano from a music teacher in the town. A site was selected in a small wood and a huge marquee was erected which contained the library etc and before it, in the middle of the clearing, was a concert platform come boxing ring with the piano beside it. The dressing-room for the artistes was a wigwam arrangement of draperies attached to the back of the piano.

The poster was produced, and it was an attractive and informative poster full of humour. The word 'lasture' should have been 'Pasture' to give the location. It can be seen that there is a wide range of activities in addition to a library, a reading and writing room for more serious activity. Beer and cigarettes are clearly important and 'even soap' is available but everyone must bring their own pots. What is interesting is that it advertises 'Dramas and Eisteddfodau' which clearly indicates a strong Welsh influence in this Scottish Battalion. An 'Eisteddfod' in Wales is a cultural event involving singing, recitation, poetry and literary competitions.

The Beer Garden opened on 27 June and it quickly became the centre of the Battalion's social life and it must have been wonderful to have such a facility in the middle of this horrific war. During the evenings, after they had been working hard digging the trenches during the day, the men would come here to relax, listen to soloists and join in the singing of the old favourites, 'Brither Scots' and 'Tipperary'. I'm sure that Tom would have made full use of the Beer Garden.

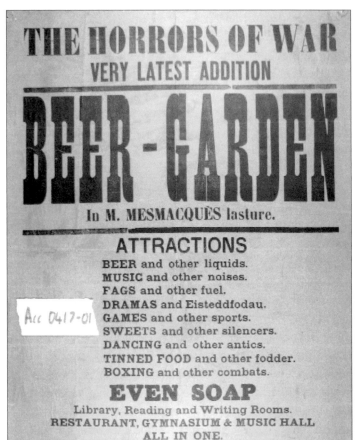

The Beer Garden opened at base camp for recreational activities

On 30 June the battalion was moved unexpectedly 4 miles south to Esquerdes but they took everything with them and the Beer Garden was reopened there, where it continued to do a thriving trade with the profits going towards the canteen funds.

On 15 July 1917 a special event was held, which McGilchrist in his book describes as the most successful entertainment ever organised by the battalion, when an eisteddfod was held in the Beer Garden. A special poster was produced and was displayed widely in the village. When I first saw this on display in the museum I expressed surprise and the curator told me that they used to call any kind of competition an 'Eisteddfod'. There was a very strong Welsh influence in Liverpool at that time which spread even into this Scottish Battalion.

The poster is fascinating, again one to attract attention and full of humour. There is the traditional male voice choir competition and the contestants for the piano solo are advised to 'examine the piano beforehand for silent keys'! The verse composition preserves the Welsh tradition of submitting entries anonymously under a pseudonym and the mouth-organ competition is understandable as this is the only musical instrument that a soldier could be expected to carry with him. I'm not sure how the Charlie Chaplin imitation and the Female Impersonations would have gone down in a traditional Welsh Eisteddfod! Note that everyone, including 'Publicans and Sinners', was invited to participate.

The Eisteddfod took place on Saturday 14 July (not the 15th, as stated on the poster) and attracted numerous entries which provided excellent entertainment. Not only were the soldiers present but the villagers also turned up in force to see the fun. Many of the village women had loaned some of their clothing to the female impersonators and they

THE BLANKTH SCOTTISH BATTALION, THE BLANKTH BLANKETY REGIMENT.

EISTEDDFOD

To be held in the Beer-Garden on
SUNDAY, JULY 15, 1917

Distinguished Patronage. Eminent Adjudicators.

CONTESTS

I. Male voice choirs.

Choirs from each company — twelve voices in each choir. Competitors to choose their own glee. Marks deducted for " Sweet and Low " and " The soldier's Farewell ".

II. Imitations of Charlie Chaplin.

Competitors are given permission to let their hair grow.

III. Whistling solos.

Indents for bird-seed should be submitted at once to the Q. M.

IV. Recitations.

As there is plenty of beer available the services of " Gunga Din " are not required.

V. Original verses.

In " Limerick " or any other form. May — or may not — be read aloud. To be sent anonymously to the Secretary, Entertainment Committee, at the Orderly Room, on or before July 13. Prizewinners must acknowledge their bantlings in public or lose their prizes.

VI. Pianoforte solos.

Operatic excerpts. Competitors should reconnoitre the piano before the attack for silent keys.

VII. Female impersonations.

Don't raid the clothes-lines. Costumes will be provided. Eve, even with foliage, is not eligible — that is, Adam's wife : the Tatler's Eve would be welcome.

VIII. Mouth-Organ contest.

Three Scottish Melodies.

IX. Comic interludes.

Any thing at all that is really funny.

Warblers, Barn-Stormers, Troubadors, Whistlers, Mountebanks, Spring Poets, Contortionists, Wine-Bibbers, Publicans and Sinners — Now is your chance.

Entries to be submitted to the company representatives on the Entertainment Committee not later than 7 p.m. on Saturday evening, July 7, 1917. These representatives are :

V Co., Serjt. THOMSON. X Co., Serjt. CODLING. Y Co., L.-Cpl. MACALISTER. Z Co., 2nd. Lieut. CLEMENTS.

H. Q. Details, L.-Cpl. J. DEWAR.

Saint-Omer, Imp. de l'Indépendant, 18, rue des Clouteries.

An Eisteddfod was held in the Beer Garden, July 1917, including some unusual categories and instructions!

were astonished by the originality displayed by some of the competitors in the way they had used the more intimate garments!

The Limerick competition was particularly popular as it gave competitors an opportunity to be both scandalous and insubordinate without the possibility of uncomfortable consequences. The only Limerick that has survived was one written by Scott Macfie himself as a model for those without the knowledge of the craft:

> Our Chief is a Colonel call Davidson,
> Who asked 'Here's a franc – if I gave it, son,
>> Would you squander the treasure
>> On women and pleasure
> Or would you be wiser and save it, son?'

I can imagine that Tom would have thoroughly enjoyed this day, along with all his comrades.

The purpose of the stay in this area was to prepare, as part of the 55th West Lancashire Division, for the biggest task that they had yet attempted. On 2 July the digging of trenches was completed and two days later training for the attack began. There was a determination that the lack of preparation shown before the Guillemont disaster in 1916 would not be repeated. On 4 July the Brigadier held a conference of officers and afterwards the Battalion and a full dress rehearsal was carried out. On 15 July a Brigade Church Parade was held in Quelmes, near Zadausques followed by a sports open to the whole brigade, where the Liverpool Scottish narrowly failed to win the championship.

Tom had not experienced real fighting since being back in France, but on 20 July 1917 the Liverpool Scottish marched to St Omer and took the train to Poperinghe. After a few hours' rest they were back again in the trenches outside Wieltje, north-east of Ypres. These trenches were familiar to the Battalion: they had been there for most of 1917 up to June – but they were new to Tom. On the night of 21/22 they were subjected to sustained bombardment of mustard-gas shells and two officers and sixty-seven men were evacuated to hospital. During the next couple of days they were subjected to heavy bombardment during the day and mustard-gas during the nights.

It was impossible to avoid casualties in a heavy concentration of this gas. The box-respirator protected the throat and eyes but the dense fumes which hung around the trenches and shell-holes attacked the skin, particularly the softer parts, and caused painful sores. The kilt was far from ideal in such circumstances.

After four difficult days, the fighting strength of the Battalion was reduced by four officers and 141 other ranks.

The Third Battle of Ypres (Passchendaele)
The Third Battle of Ypres is considered to have started officially on 31 July 1917. On the evening of 29 July fighting stores were issued at 8.00 pm and the Battalion of twenty-five officers and 475 other ranks marched off to their assembly positions which they reached by 12.50 am on 30 July. This was an exhausting march as they were carrying two days' full food rations in addition to the battle requirements. They rested during the night and during the following day when movement was kept to a minimum in order to reduce the risk of the enemy detecting the great concentration of troops.

At 8.30 pm on 30 July the companies moved up to the jumping off trenches and were all in position by midnight. They had no camouflage to conceal their position and they came under heavy fire. At 3.50 am on 31 July they moved forward to engage the enemy and did so successfully during the remainder of the night and during the day. By the end of 31 July they had advanced considerably.

The morning of 31 July had been dry but it started raining heavily from noon onwards, and the rain continued throughout the night and during the day of 1 August. By the evening the new trenches had filled with water and the walls were collapsing. The men had to be taken out of these trenches, but even then they managed to disperse the enemy before the enemy could take advantage of the situation.

The Liverpool Scottish was relieved of front line duty in the early hours of 3 August following a highly successful attack demonstrating the value of preliminary training. Again they paid a heavy price, with four officers and fifty-one other ranks killed and eight officers and 172 other ranks wounded, and sixteen men missing. However, they had the satisfaction of knowing that they had caused the enemy much heavier permanent losses and they felt that they had made up for the failure at Guillemont in 1916.

There were many examples of exceptional courage and bravery, one of whom was, once again, the Medical Officer Capt. Noel Chavasse who went out to rescue injured men. He exceeded his own past record of courage and self-sacrifice which saw him awarded the VC at Guillemont. Whilst carrying a wounded man to his dressing station early on 31 July he was severely wounded on the right side of the head. The other officers implored him to go back to get his wound attended to but he refused. The next day, 1 August, he was again hit, this time on the left side of his head. He still insisted on carrying out his duties and did not confine his work to his dressing station as he repeatedly went out with stretcher-parties to the firing-line to dress those lying out and to carry badly wounded men back under heavy fire. Though suffering intense pain he continued for two days during which he had no rest and very little food.

On the morning of 2 August, as he was dressing a wounded man, a shell hit his dressing-station and he

Capt Noel Chavasse and the memorial to him in Abercromby Square, Liverpool

received a terrible body wound. He was taken to hospital and operated upon but his case was hopeless and he died on 4 August. He was awarded a Bar to his VC and a second VC; he was the only man to be awarded two VCs during WW1 and only one of three people ever to achieve this distinction. More than once he was offered the less dangerous work at a Casualty Clearing Station or Field Hospital, to which his long service as a regimental medical officer entitled him, but he preferred to remain with the men he knew and admired.

There is a memorial to Noel Chavasse at Brandhoek Church near Ypres in Belgium. There is a statue in Abercromby Square in Liverpool, which also features a Liverpool Scottish stretcher-bearer and a casualty, and also a 'blue' plaque. There are also plaques in Liverpool College, Mosley Hill, and also in Trinity College, Oxford, together with a smaller version of the Abercromby Square statue.

Many other awards were also made: one Distinguished Service Order, five Military Crosses, two Distinguished Conduct Medals and twenty-two Military Medals, including two Bars to existing MMs won at Hooge and Guillemont. The Liverpool Scottish had certainly distinguished themselves. Tom was involved in this action but I have no details.

Hedd Wyn

Many Welsh readers will know that 31 July 1917 was the day that the bard Hedd Wyn (Elis Humphrey Evans of Trawsfynydd) lost his life at Pilckem Ridge, in the Passchendaele battle. During home leave he had started his entry for the Chair competition at the Welsh National Eisteddfod, and he completed it when he rejoined the Royal Welsh Fusiliers in France. He posted his entry on 15 July and was killed sixteen days later. When the Eisteddfod was held on 6 September Hedd Wyn was declared the posthumous winner; the winner's empty chair was dramatically draped with a black sheet. It is still remembered as 'the Eisteddfod of the black chair'.

The Liverpool Scottish move on

The Liverpool Scottish left the area on 4 August and eventually arrived in Zouafques, a village in a wooded valley about half way between St Omer and Calais. During early August new drafts of seven officers and 500 men joined the battalion. Fortunately they had a month at Zouafques to assimilate the new arrivals and to retrain. On 10 September there was a divisional exercise to test and evaluate the new training. On 3 September Col. Davidson returned home and was replaced as Commanding Officer by Major MacDonald who had been in command during the fighting from 31 July to 3 August and was well known and well respected by the Battalion.

The Battalion moved on 13 September to Goldfish Château not far from Ypres. Here they were given the task of capturing some enemy posts on the banks of the river Hanebeek and on the night of 17 September they succeeded in capturing the positions after some fighting. On the night of 19 September the Liverpool Scottish moved through heavy rain to the assembly position for the next offensive. Following considerable fighting they were relieved at midnight on 22 September, having lost eleven men killed and forty wounded. In this case they considered themselves lucky to have got off so lightly.

By this time the Liverpool Scottish had been in France for two years and ten months, of which all but some ten months had been spent in or on the fringe of the Ypres Salient. It is believed that no other battalion in the British Army could claim such a long period of service in what was considered to be the worst portion of the whole front.

On 23 September the Battalion started on a move south ending up in Villiers-Faucon, to the north of Saint-Quentin and to the south of Cambrai. By 30 September they were occupying trenches in front of Epéhy near the Hindenburg Line, the line to which the German forces had withdrawn from the Somme in spring 1917. This defensive line was considered to be impenetrable.

One curious aspect of the Epéhy trenches was that they seemed to attract all the frogs in the neighbourhood. The Battalion was well used to rats in the trenches, but frogs were a new experience. They seemed to hide during the day but swarmed out at night and became a danger to those walking the duckboards in the dark. They were as slippery as stepping on a banana skin and made an unpleasant popping sound as they were squashed.

The Battalion was relieved on 18 October and received training for ten days before going back to the lines on 28 October. Tom's Y Company was based in Pigeon Quarry, which had been well fitted out and contained a rare bath house with hot showers. The military drawback was that there were only two exits which made the occupants vulnerable if trying to leave under fire. They were now in position to take part in the Battle of Cambrai.

The Battle of Cambrai

Following the German withdrawal from the Somme in Spring 1917 the 'Hindenburg Line became the strongly fortified front line which was considered to be impenetrable. Cambrai was an important railhead and HQ behind the German lines. Sir Julian Byng, commanding the Third Army, went to see Field Marshal Sir Douglas Haig in August to ask that he be allowed to make a surprise attack on Cambrai and plans were developed.

During the first two years of the war the use of the tank had not been the great success that had been hoped for. They had been part of the Machine Gun Corps and known as the 'Heavy Branch' before the 'Tank Corps' was established as a separate unit on 27 July 1917. Under their commander, Brigadier-General Hugh Elles and his Chief of Staff, Colonel John Fuller they were free to develop their own strategies. The Tank Corps strongly supported the attack on Cambrai as the ground in this area was far more suitable for tanks than the previous battlefields which were full of bomb craters and trenches.

The artillery was also keen to try out a new approach of unregistered artillery. Previously an artillery bombardment at the start an offensive had to be preceded by initial firing in order to establish the target accurately. This action, of course, removed the element of surprise in the actual attack. During 1917 there had been developments in the technology and it was considered that they could now determine targets without having to carryout preliminary firing. They had been practicing and were eager for an opportunity to try out their new strategy in a real attack.

There was therefore a body of support for a surprise attack on Cambrai although there were many with doubts. Subsequent investigations show that the plans had been improvised and inadequately prepared.

The map shows the battle lines for the Battle of Cambrai showing the German Hindenburg Line and the British line before the attack. Epéhy is seen in the south-east corner of the map some 2 miles from the British lines where the Liverpool Scottish was now engaged. Just in front of the German lines in this area was the St Quentin Canal, which the British would have to cross. Note the village of Honnecourt north-east of Epéhy between the British and German lines as this will become important later. Plans were issued on 13 November to take surprise and rapid action to break through the previously considered impenetrable Hindenburg Line and then make rapid progress to surround and isolate Cambrai and cut off the rail connections.

The preparations were successful in moving some 1,000 artillery guns into position for the attack without detection by the enemy. Similarly 476 tanks had been moved into the attack position without detection. Aircraft had been flying around to mask the sounds of the movement of tanks. Everything was ready for the surprise attack.

The attack was launched at 6.20 am on 20 November

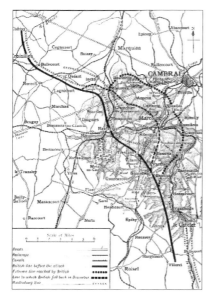

Maps of the battle of Cambrai

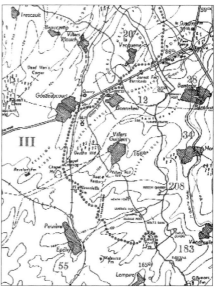

1917, and took the enemy by complete surprise. The tanks advanced through the Hindenburg Line and the infantry followed and made good progress. One of the bridges across the St Quentin Canal was important for the cavalry to cross but unfortunately the first tank to cross, known as the *Flying Fox*, was too heavy and broke the back of the bridge. This considerably hampered the cavalry advance with the result that they subsequently failed in their objective of surrounding Cambrai. There was considerable fighting over the following days but on 27 November orders came to close down the offensive operations and to consolidate the positions. The map shows that despite the failure to surround and isolate Cambrai that a considerable advance had been made, shown by the dotted line. They had also demonstrated that the Hindenburg Line could be penetrated.

The Germans had suffered heavy losses in the initial attacks but then started to reorganise and build up reinforcements. By 27 November they had considerably built up their forces and were in a position to plan a counter attack. The German Plan was to cut the neck of the salient by attacking each side at the base of the salient in order to try to surround the British on the front line so that they could be attacked from both sides. The strongest blow was to be on the southern side which was being defended by the 55th West Lancashire Division which included the Liverpool Scottish.

The counter-attack came on 30 November at 7.30 am and was devastatingly effective. By 9.00 am the Germans had penetrated almost 3 miles across the British lines on the southern side, with the 55th West Lancashire Division taking the full brunt of the attack.

The more detailed map of the Epéhy area is shown. The Liverpool Scottish Y Company, to which Tom belonged, was based at Pigeon Quarry, which can be seen on the map near the figure '208', and Z Company in nearby Cox's Bank. Prior to the attack there was an intense German bombardment at 7.00 am, which broke telephone communications, and from that time no messages were received from Y and Z Companies. Four men from these Companies, three of them wounded, got back to Battalion HQ, but it was not until after the war that anything was known of what had happened to these two companies. They had effectively disappeared from the Battalion records for the rest of the war!

Subsequent accounts show that the battalions on the front line were overwhelmed in the initial German attack , leaving the Liverpool Scottish totally exposed. Y Company went out of Pigeon Quarry towards the front line but, following bitter fighting, decided to make their way back to the quarry but they then found themselves surrounded and the men and the wounded had no choice but to surrender.

The wiping out of Y and Z Companies left the rest of the battalion with a completely exposed flank and added considerably to the difficulties of holding an inadequately prepared and undermined position. There was considerable bitter fighting before the Liverpool Scottish was relieved at 4.00 am on 2 December.

The Liverpool Scottish casualties as first given were eleven men killed or died of wounds, nine officers and sixty-seven other ranks wounded, with nine officers and 435 other ranks missing – amongst whom were members of Y and Z Companies. Of the missing it was found that one officer and ninety men had been killed. The remainder turned up over time in prisoner-of-war camps in Germany. Amongst these was Tom, who had been shot in the left thigh and taken prisoner. Tom's war record is not very legible but shows that he was taken prisoner at Honnecourt, which can be seen on the edge of the map just above the 208 figure. This was the nearest village to Pigeon Quarry which fits in with the account that the men surrendered on the way back to Pigeon Quarry.

Between 20 November and 8 December the Third Army reported losses of dead, wounded and missing of 44,207 men. Of these some 6,000 were taken prisoner during the enemy counter-attack on 30 November. Enemy casualties for the same period were estimated at approximately 45,000. These are truly frightening figures.

The Cambrai initiative was certainly innovative but it failed to achieve its objectives and many considered it to be a dismal defeat due to inadequate planning. Questions were raised in the War Cabinet and an official inquiry was conducted two months later. Many lessons were learnt which were valuable to the conduct of the war during 1918.

8
1917-1918
Prisoner-of-War Camp

Tom had been shot in the left thigh. Following capture near
Honnecourt on 30 November 1917, Tom must have
received hospital treatment in Germany but there is nothing
in his official records to say where this took place. Had his
letters home been kept they would probably have contained
this information. He eventually ended up in a prisoner-of-
war camp in Minden, but again there is no official date when
this happened, or in how many camps he was placed before
ending up in Minden. As the Battalion had no records of
what had happened to Y Company I assume that fairly soon
after 30 November 1917 his father would have received

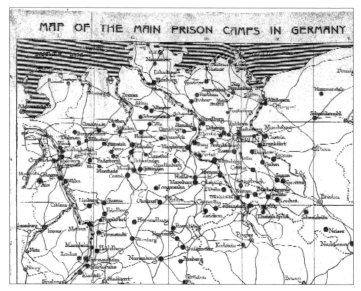

Map of the main prisoner-of-war camps in Germany and Austria, with some in
what is now Poland

notification that he was missing. I often wonder how long it took before his family in Penmachno learnt that he was alive in the camp. That period of uncertainty must have been so painful and was suffered by so many families during this cruel war.

It's almost unbelievable how many prisoner-of-war camps there were in Germany and Austria; many also had associated subsidiary camps! Minden is in the north of Germany on the river Waser. Tom's photo album contained twenty-three photos taken inside the POW camp and these are quite rare. There are a number of photos of other prisoners which would suggest that they were exchanging photographs as keepsakes. Some of these fortunately have names and addresses on the back.

There are six head-and-shoulder photos in the same format which suggest that these are the official photos taken on entry to the camp. Below is Tom's official photo, and also a photo of the official camp stamp which appears on the back of most of the photos. This reads: '*Photographic genehming Kommandanur des Gefangenenlargers Minden*' showing that the photograph has been officially approved.

There are four similar photos of British soldiers with names and addresses on the back:

> Pte. C Tenant, Royal Scots, 12 Marlow Rd, Homerton, London
> Pte. Peter M Namee, 8th Royal Inniskilling Fusilliers.
> James J Fearn, 2nd Bn, The Royal Scots, 15 Avenue Road, Springham, Glasgow
> Jas Cunningham, 13th Bn, The Royal Scots, 82 Dunchahathan, Deniston, Glasgow (dated 1 October 1918)

Six photographs taken in the Minden prisoner-of-war camp, with the official stamp of approval: Tom

Photographie genehmigt
Kommandantur des
Gefangenenlagers Minden

Official approval

Pte. C. Tenant, London

Pte. Peter M Namee, Iniskillen

James J. Fearn, Glasgow

Jas. Cunningham, Glasgow

Victor Dankin, France

*Three more prisoner-of-war
photographs – unidentified men*

Tom was clearly friendly with Scots and the Irish prisoners; the sixth similar photo is of Victor Dankin, a French prisoner who also appears in other photos. Tom's knowledge of French must have been of particular value to him during his period of service. It became even more important in the POW camp where there were French-speaking prisoners as well as many other nationalities.

The next photo shows three British prisoners with the name F W Rhodes of 168 Brunswick Road, Sheffield, written on the back but no indication which one he is. There is a group of eleven soldiers from different

Victor Dankin and friend

Tagner Louis, France

Mikhael Nikoforov, Russia

nationalities. Then we have two soldiers, but from which country?

The next photo shows Victor again, this time in a field, with a friend, presumably doing farm work. They are both smoking, so they managed to get cigarettes from home.

Then two photos with names and addresses written on the back – a French officer named Taugner Louis and a Russian named Mikhael Nikoforov.

Philippe seen in the next photo must have been a close friend as he's written 'To my friend Williams'.

'Souvenir of our time in captivity', from Tom's friend Philippe

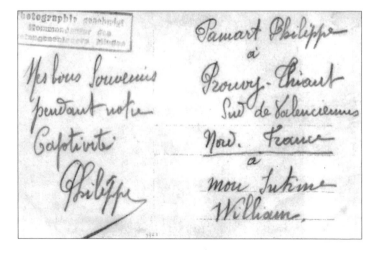

Presumably they would have been known by their surnames in the camp. The back of the photo shows the camp stamp clearly and Philippe has written his full name and address with a highly emotive message, 'A souvenir of our time in captivity'. Presumably this would have been written at the time when they knew that they would be leaving the camp for home. This was probably the time when most of the photographs were exchanged.

Five photographs given to Tom by Russian fellow prisoners-of-war

There is a photo of an individual Russian, Feklinov Pravkofy, and there are individual photos of three other unnamed Russians. The name of one of the two Russians is Vladimir Zurichov with an address in Pozharevski. There are two photos of groups of six Russians with the name Peter Fokin written on the back of the first and then there is a group of sixteen Russians. All these photos indicate that Tom was friendly with the Russian prisoners.

The next photograph is of a group of twenty-three Russians. This is a remarkable postcard, the back of which is

Undelivered postcard, which fell foul of a 'breakdown in communications' between a Russian prisoner and his wife. This 'breakdown in communication' was caused by the Russian Revolution

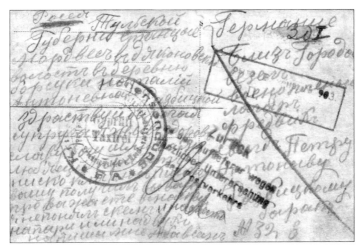

shown. It is written in Russian, has an address in Russia, and has been stamped three times. Although the wording can't be seen, the rectangular stamp is the official camp stamp. There is a circular stamp which states that no postage is required as this is a POW communication. The third stamp states that the card cannot be delivered because of a breakdown in communications. By this time the revolution had broken out in Russia – hence the 'breakdown in communications' – and the card was returned to the camp.

The card has been written in the Russian style of the period, which I understand is very different to modern Russian. It has been written by one of the group to his wife, Natalvijg Antonevna Razbickayer, and starts, 'Hello my dear wife, I'm alive and healthy thanks to God ...' This card did not get delivered and I wonder when this wife actually learnt that her husband was alive. People in Russia were going through the turmoil of the revolution, as well as having no idea of what was happening to their loved ones in Germany.

There is a question whether or not this man ever saw his wife after the war. Most of the Russians serving in the army were 'white' Russians and didn't go back to Russia after the war because they were afraid of being punished by the 'red' Russians now in charge. It's remarkable that this photo found its way into Tom's photo album. Tom must have been a good friend to this Russian. Another factor could be that the Russians were not receiving any pay from home because of the revolution and were selling the photos to get cash.

Tom sent an official camp postcard to my mother dated 6 April 1918. It has the camp name on the top and Tom has written the address for the reply on the bottom left; this suggests that there were subsidiary camps or work stations to which correspondence could be sent.

> Dear All Just a few lines to let you know that I have moved from Friedrichsfeld sooner than expected to the farming centre and also I have turned to be a farmer which is a great change from tailoring but one gets used to everything and so far all is well. Please put my regimental number and camp number on all letters. You will notice that I have a new camp number, which is the

Postcard to Kate from the prisoner-of-war camp (Tom is second from right in the back row), with caption: 'Some jolly boys of Wales'

custom when changing to various Lager's. Look out for some lessons in farming when I shall return which I hope won't be long. Yours etc T Wms.

The last reference to lessons in farming is a joke for his brother who was a farmer! It seems that Tom had kept his sense of humour in the POW camp. This shows that he had recovered sufficiently from his injuries for him to be sent out to work. He is also hopeful that the end of the war would not be too long.

From this card it is clear that Tom also spent time at the Friedrichsfeld camp, which is a long way from Minden, but there is nothing on his records to indicate this. How long was he at the Friedrichsfeld camp and when did he go there? Was it common for prisoners to be moved between POW camps?

On 12 May 1918 Tom sent a remarkable postcard showing a group of twenty-three prisoners in uniform with the caption 'Some Jolly Boys of Wales'. Tom is second from the right in the back row but is wearing a cap that is certainly not that of the Liverpool Scottish. One of the first things that the curator of the Liverpool Scottish Museum told me was, 'He's certainly not wearing one of our caps'. They look as if they were in a Butlins Holiday Camp! This was probably a propaganda initiative by the German authorities to try to reassure people back home that prisoners were being well looked after. The message on the back addressed to my mother, then aged nine, says 'Just to let you know that so far I am alright, trusting that you are the same.' I also have a blank copy of this card.

At least twenty-three homes in Wales received this postcard and I've been trying unsuccessfully to find out whether another copy still exists today. I published the photo and an article in *Gwreiddiau Gwynedd*, the journal of the Gwynedd Family History Society, and the Dyfed FHS journal also carried an article and the photo. It appeared in a number of local weekly newspapers and also Welsh language community newspapers in Wales, without any response.

I had more success through the Rootsweb Mailing Lists. These are web-based messaging lists used widely by family history researchers and are based on the traditional counties. People send messages to these lists asking if anyone has information about individuals or events hoping that someone on the list has useful information. I placed messages on each of the Wales lists and those covering the UK addresses that had appeared on the photographs. I received some feedback from these but I had far more success when I went on to the Great War Forum website which has various sections including one on POWs.

One respondent to my posting of this photo on the Great War Forum said that there was:

> a fascinating variety of cap badges on display. There are a couple of Monmouthshire Regt. men and a

South Wales Borderer, and perhaps several Royal Welsh Fusiliers. The rest seem to be Dorset Regt., Royal Berkshire Regt., Middlesex Regt., Coldstream (& possibly Grenadier) Guards, and one or two whose outline is unfamiliar.

A few years ago I maintained a Family History Blog on the website of our local newspaper, the *Caernarfon Herald*, and in response to posting a photo of the 'Jolly Boys' I was delighted to get a message from Brian Hollins who said 'I believe that the man in the centre of the second row could well be my grandfather Sgt. William John Garland of the 1st Bn. Monmouthshire Regt. He was POW in Friedrichsfeld from 1915 until 1918. He was captured in Frenzenburg.' One other person in the photo has been identified – only twenty-one left now!

It was this response that made me realise that the 'Jolly Boys' photo had most likely been taken at the Friedrichsfeld camp and not at Minden. Tom had been there until early April and the card had been posted from Minden in early May.

One of the questions which puzzled me was how the photographs taken in the POW camps were paid for, particularly those that had been made to be used as postcards. I can understand that photos such as the 'Jolly Boys' photo would have been paid for by the German authorities as they had a propaganda purpose, but what about the others? There was an interesting contribution from Doug Johnston on the Great War Forum in October 2009 on what happened to POWs' army pay whilst they were prisoners. When soldiers were declared missing their pay would be kept until it was established what had happened to them. If they were in a POW camp British prisoners could elect to have it paid to their family back home or paid to themselves in the camp or probably a proportion to both. Prisoners were also paid for work they undertook in Germany, and it's understood that some skilled workers received a good rate of pay from their German employers. It is therefore possible that the prisoners themselves were paying for some photographs.

The Armistice was signed on 11 November 1918 but Tom's record shows that he was not released from the POW camp until 21 December 1918. Unfortunately the most important date – of his arrival at Minden – is unclear and impossible to read.

There is no information from Tom as to the conditions he experienced in the camps. Conditions varied considerably between individual camps and the little information that I've seen claimed that Friedrichsfeld was considered to be a good camp but unfortunately conditions in Minden were not considered to be good. Yet the majority of the photographs, other than the 'Jolly Boys', carry the Minden stamp on the back. I can only hope that Tom was not mistreated.

An outline of the activities of the Liverpool Scottish December 1917 to November 1918

Following the Battle of Cambrai the Liverpool Scottish were relieved from the front line on 2 December 1917. They moved several times during December, including undertaking a number of days marching, and ended up the village of Beaumets-lez-Aire some 20 miles west of Béthune in northern France, where they spent Christmas.

An important and beneficial innovation was introduced in January 1918. Those who had been in continuous service in the line for two years or were suffering from strain or for very urgent private reasons could be eligible for six months' home leave. Those granted the much-needed leave had to be recommended by commanding officers and had to be replaced by others of similar rank from draft-finding units at home.

In February 1918 they were moved again ending up in Le Préol near the Aire–La Bassée Canal some two miles from the front line. On 25 February they were back in the trenches in front of Givenchy some 6 miles north of Arras. There had been action here in December 1914 but there had been very little movement on this line since 1915 and the defences were highly organised. Givenchy was nothing more than a heap of rubble. They were relieved from the line on 4 March.

By this time the Germans were reinforcing along this front with divisions set free by the collapse of the Russians on the Eastern front. An attack was therefore expected, but where? The British undertook extensive work on an elaborate defence scheme. The attack came on 21 March on the southern portion of the line with sweeping success which indicated further attacks elsewhere.

The Liverpool Scottish was back in the trenches when the Battle of Givenchy started on 9 April 1918. Severe enemy bombardment started at 3.30 a.m. and knocked out the Divisional Artillery, which was exposed because they had been built up rather than dug down. Severe fighting continued and the battalion was relieved from the line on the night of 15/16 April. The losses were two officers and fifty-seven other men killed, eight officers and 127 others wounded, with one officer and five others missing, who were later reported killed. The Battalion had again distinguished itself and numerous decorations were awarded.

Following this strenuous action they didn't have much rest as they were back in the trenches again on 20 April before being relieved on 27 April. The casualties this time were two officers and twenty-four others killed and fifty men wounded.

The activities of the Liverpool Scottish reported so far in this book have been those of the First Battalion. There was also a Second Battalion which had been at home until coming to France on 24 February 1917 and they participated in the action in the Armentieres Sector. On 30 April 1918 they were officially amalgamated with the First Battalion at Vadricourt, some two miles south of Béthune, and they served as one combined battalion for the remainder of the war.

They returned to the trenches on 2 May, with periodic rests but did not see much significant activity during the months up to September. On 2 October the enemy was seen to be starting to withdraw and preparations were made for the British advance. On 3 October the advance started with the Liverpool Scottish in the front line. They were relieved on 5 October with one officer and nineteen others killed, four officers and fifty-five others wounded and forty-five missing. Again several decorations were awarded.

At 6.30 a.m. on 16 October they started to move to the Marquillies area and on 17 October they moved forward in pursuit of the enemy. They found deserted villages which had been subjected to wanton and malicious destruction and looting as the enemy retreated. They marched eastwards and after a couple of days they found undamaged villages as the enemy had been in too much of a hurry to destroy them. They started to see civilians and on 20 October the villages were decorated with bunting and national and allied flags and the streets were lined with cheering, laughing and hysterical people who hardly knew what to do to express their joy. The Liverpool Scottish was the first kilted battalion that the people had ever seen, which caused great excitement, and the Pipe Band had never before had such an enthusiastic audience!

Up to 20 October there was no serious opposition, but on 21 October there was severe resistance and it was clear that the enemy was going to make a stand. The next few days passed without incident other than for the heavy bombardment, particularly during the nights. On 25 October the Liverpool Scottish became the outpost battalion and subjected to regular shelling and one man was killed and four wounded. On 30 October they were drenched with mustard gas and many had to be sent to the dressing-station for attention. On this day they were interested spectators to a thrilling air-battle and they saw, for the first time, a pilot jumping out of a plane and using a parachute.

They were relieved on 31 October and that night came the news that Turkey had signed an armistice and the next day Austria had capitulated. The end was in sight. They returned to the lines on 5 November and plans were made to attack, but on the morning of 8 November the enemy was seen to be withdrawing and they were energetically pursued. Later that night news came that the Germans had been given until 11.00 a.m. on 11 November to accept an armistice.

On the morning of 9 November the Liverpool Scottish left their billets to move forward again and crossed the Belgian border. The following day they set off with the Pipe Band to the town of Barry east of Tournai and then on to Leuze where they had the most wonderful welcome with the entire population turning out to greet them including monks and nuns.

By the evening of 10 November they had reached the Dentre River and the Blaton Canal which was held by the enemy. Plans were made to attack in the morning of 11 November. But news came to the HQ of the imminent armistice at 11.00 am. As the Liverpool Scottish waited for the orders to attack they received a visit from the commanding officer who told them that he had seen the official news that the armistice had been signed. Troops and civilians at once went mad. All the church bells in the district were set ringing, and the Pipe Band marched up and down the village streets through crowds of cheering troops and excited locals.

The war was over.

9
1918
Coming Home

In his postcard sent in April 1918 Tom was expressing his view that it would not be long before he was home but the

Postcard from Enschede in The Netherlands, 16 December 1918, telling Kate that her Uncle Tom will soon be back in England

armistice was not signed until 11 November. He, and his fellow prisoners, must have been overjoyed at the news but the wait until they were released to be sent home must have been excruciatingly frustrating. The official record shows that the date of departure from the camp was 21 December 1918 which was nearly six weeks after the armistice was signed.

Tom sent a postcard to my mother from Enschede in Holland on his way home dated 16 December 1918 so he must have left the camp before this date. It appears that the date on his official record was not the date he left the camp but the date on which he left Europe. Nevertheless it was a month following the armistice before he left the camp. On the card he writes:

> Dear All. Arrived here yesterday (Holland) and very probably will be in England in a few days. Pleased to say that I am in the pink. Tom.

I'm not surprised that he was feeling 'in the pink'!

Official documents issued during this period

On arriving in the UK on 22 December he was sent to the POW Reception Camp, Ripon, Yorkshire. Amongst his records on Ancestry is a copy of a two-month furlough, with rail warrants, that was granted to returning POWs. This was issued at Ripon, although unfortunately the date of issue is unclear. It's assumed that there were formalities, including medical examinations, to be completed at Ripon before the two-month leave was authorised. The 'Statement of Officer or Soldier as to Wound' document was completed and signed at Ripon. The date on the leave form is unclear but it could be 30 December 1918. It can therefore be assumed that Tom was on leave during January and February 1919.

The date of 30 December is confirmed by a report in the North Wales Weekly News published on 2 January 1919 with the heading 'RETURNED PRISONER OF WAR' stating:

> Pte Tom Williams, Liverpool Scottish, who before the war was employed as a cutter with Mr H R Davies of Abergele Road, has returned from Germany where he was a prisoner since November 30th 1917. He was badly wounded at Cambrai.

Amongst his official documents, one document is totally unclear apart from the words 'Ration Book N57 037872' so Tom must have been issued with a Ration Book during this period. All Tom's official correspondence was sent to his father's home in Penmachno, but he must have been spending most of his time in Colwyn Bay during January and February, as postcards postmarked Colwyn Bay sent on 31 January and 26 February 1919 show. Both cards say that he will be in Penmachno on the following Saturday. One can assume that he had contact with his employer and work colleagues at H. R. Davies and other friends.

Another of the official documents is a letter from H. R. Davies. Only the letterhead, date and Tom's army number are legible, together with a Ministry of Labour stamp at the bottom. This is dated 24 February 1919 and I assume that this is a letter from his former employer confirming that he will be re-employed on his discharge from the army.

Another document issued at this time was the 'Protection Certificate and Certificate of Identity (Soldier not remaining with the colours)' dated 28 February 1919. This grants Tom a 28-day furlough presumably until the end of his service, so Tom's leave was now extended through March. This gives the address for pay to be sent as Gwiga,

Penmachno, and he acknowledges the receipt of an advance of £2. At the bottom of the Certificate there's a statement: 'This Certificate must be produced when applying for an Unemployed Sailors and Soldiers Donation Policy or, if demanded, whenever applying for Unemployment benefit'. However, Tom was employed immediately on discharge, so he never had to seek unemployment benefit.

The Unemployed Sailors' and Soldiers' Donation Policy was a free insurance introduced in November 1918, against unemployment for a year in the case of discharged soldiers or sailors, and for six months in the case of civilians. Men for whom work could not be found received 24 shillings a week, and women 20 shillings a week, with allowances for dependent children under fifteen of 6 shillings for the first child and 3 shillings for each additional child. An unemployed man with three young children would thus receive 36 shillings a week. A government statement at the time said:

> The public, we are sure, feels that it is impossible to do too much for the relief of our gallant sailors and soldiers, and in a lesser degree of the patriotic minition-workers, who may find themselves temporarily unemployed. Prudence as well as gratitude requires the generous treatment of those who have deserved well of the State. At the same time the scheme must be administered with great care. Loafers must not be encouraged to live at the State's expense, and decent men and women must be found employment with the least possible delay, for nothing is more demoralising than enforced idleness.

An important document is that issued by the Ministry of Pensions which gives his date of discharge as 25 March 1919 and his address at discharge as Gwiga, Penmachno. It records his wounded left hip as a disability that was attributable to the war and states that his degree of disablement was 20 per cent. He was awarded a weekly pension of 5s 6d. as from 26 March 1919 to be reviewed in fifty-two weeks. There are no records to show whether or not his pension was continued after the fifty-two weeks. There is also a document to acknowledge receipt for this statement of disability.

There is an Army document 'Certificate of Disembodiment on Demobilisation' also dated 25 February 1919, which interestingly states that Tom was authorised on 11 November 1918 to receive medals and decorations. It also gives the 'place of re-joining in case of emergency' as Oswestry, which gives him a clear indication that if there was an emergency Tom would have to re-join the army.

There are two completely unreadable documents and one form for details of marriage and children which has clearly been left unfilled. There is a copy of the 'Territorial Force Attestation' and also the 'Imperial and General Service Obligation' both of which Tom signed when he enlisted on 21 November 1915. There is a Statement of Service which summaries his record as they occur and this states that he was discharged as being 'surplus to Military requirements having suffered impairment since entry into the Service'. There is also a Military History Sheet which summarises his service. Tom spent three years and 125 days in the army but from 26 March 1919 he was back at work as a salesman and cutter with H. R. Davies, Tailor, Abergele Road, Colwyn Bay.

Another document from this period is dated 15 May requesting the return of the 'Certificate in respect of your transfer to the Army Reserve', which confirms that Tom remained listed as a Reservist. This is date stamped 27 May 1919 which is presumably the date that the Infantry Record Office in Preston received the returned Certificate.

Medals Awarded

On 29 September 1920 Tom has signed for the receipt of the Silver War Badge and Certificate numbered 488756 from the Infantry Record Office in Preston. This badge was issued to officers and men who were discharged or retired from the military forces as a result of sickness or injury caused by their war service. After April 1918 this eligibility was extended to include civilians serving with the Royal Army Medical Corps. Each badge was engraved with the unique number on the certificate but unfortunately Tom's Badge has not survived and neither has the certificate.

Silver War Badge, given to all who had been retired from the forces due to war injury. Tom received one of these, but it has not survived

On 18 April 1922 Tom was sent his British War Medal and the Allied Victory Medal and I'm pleased that both have been kept safely. The ribbons which originally accompanied these medals have unfortunately not survived. The British War Medal 1914–1918 was awarded to all officers and men of the British and Imperial Forces who entered service overseas between 5 August 1914 and 11 November 1918. Approximately 6.4 million of these silver medals were issued, which indicates the frightening numbers who participated in this war.

The Allied Victory Medal depicts a winged classical figure representing victory and the reverse has the words 'The Great War for Civilisation'. Approximately 5.7 million

British War Medal, awarded to all who had served in the War

of these victory medals were issued. Whilst Tom received his Silver War Badge in September 1920 these medals did not arrive until eighteen months later. The reason for this delay was probably because the rim of both of these medals was impressed individually with the recipient's service

Tom's name engraved on his War Medal

number, rank, name and unit. The photo of the rim of the British War Medal shows 'Pte. T. Williams', the full inscription is '5707 Pte. T. Williams L'pool R'. Including this individual information on each medal was an enormous task and this was not done on the general medals issued following WW2. These medals were affectionally known at the time as Squeak and Wilfred respectively, based on comic strip characters published in the *Daily Mirror*. Sadly Tom's father had died in February 1922 so he never saw Tom's medals.

Amongst Tom's possessions is the small badge shown, which has been kept in a small box and is in an excellent condition. This was not an official badge and was known as a 'sweetheart's brooch', which were made in various forms, by different manufacturers. They were sold to raise funds in order to purchase so-called

A small 'sweetheart's brooch', sold to raise funds for 'luxuries' for the troops

'luxury' items for the troops at the front such as balaclavas, gloves, gum-boots, chocolate etc.

Peace Treaty and Peace Day

The Treaty of Versailles, the Peace Treaty that ended the war between Germany and the Allied Powers, was signed on 28 June 1919. This explains why many people refer to the war as the Great War 1914–1919 whilst others refer to it as the Great War 1914–1918 which the period of actual fighting. This led to the announcement of an official Peace Day on 19 July 1919 which was declared a Public Holliday throughout the United Kingdom.

In Colwyn Bay a Committee of sixty-eight people, with the support of the Borough Council, organised the Colwyn Bay Peace Celebrations on this day, with details outlined in an official programme priced 2d. The day starts with a bilingual Public Service at 10.30 a.m. in the Pier Pavilion. At 12.30 p.m. children received Peace Souvenir Medals. I haven't seen any examples of the Colwyn Bay medals but other towns produced medals which featured their coat of arms. The children then proceed to Pendorlan Field ready to join a procession starting at 2.00 p.m. The Procession was led by a band followed by Magistrates, Councillors, the Committee, representatives of numerous Societies, the Fire Brigade, Sunday Schools and finally the Brotherhood. The programme lists thirty-seven Sunday Schools in the district; I wonder how many function today in 2014. They proceeded through the town from East Parade to the Cayley Promenade, where a further bilingual service was held with two hymns and two addresses followed by the two national anthems.

At 4.00 p.m. the gathering dispersed to various schools for tea which was free for scholars under eighteen, Teachers and persons over seventy years of age. At 5.30 p.m. there was free entertainment for children aged under fourteen and adults aged over seventy, which took place in a number of centres: the Public Hall Theatre, Conway Road Cinema, Princess Theatre, Rhos Playhouse, Victoria Pier and Pavilion and Catlin's Arcadia.

Between 6.00 and 8.00 p.m. there was a full Sports Programme and Amusements following which flares were lit on Penmaen Head and Bryn Euryn. There was then a firework display on the Caley promenade and seafront.

The *North Wales Weekly News* on 24 July reported that there were huge crowds watching the parade at every site and that all the events were fully supported. One item which caught my eye was a quotation from the address, in Welsh, by the Rev. Thomas Parry, who declared: 'Mr Lloyd George is God's gift to the nation (loud cheers), and let us thank God for him.' This sums up the adulation that existed at that time, in Wales in particular, for Lloyd George.

Tom would have thoroughly enjoyed this day as would the majority of the residents. However, there were people who were opposed to the expense of the celebrations. The Colwyn Bay branch of the Discharged and Demobilised Soldiers and Sailors Federation had sent a letter to the Borough Council protesting against:

> spending of public funds on Peace Celebrations whilst disabled men, widows and dependents of men who have fallen are receiving pensions totally inadequate to meet the cost of living, and nearly half a million men are vainly seeking employment. We are therefore reluctantly compelled to take no official part in the Peace Celebrations in Colwyn Bay and withdraw our representatives from the Committee.

One can understand this viewpoint and the letter indicates the huge problems that many families were facing at the end of the war. Tom was lucky in that his previous employer had given him his job back on discharge from the army. The Chairman of the Council noted the intention to prepare special entertainment for the ex-servicemen at a later date and this promise was printed in the programme.

During September 1919 the Colwyn Bay Borough Council set up a committee to prepare a 'worthy reception' for ex-service men from the area, an estimated 2,000. Preparations were made to hold it on Tuesday 11 November 1919 to coincide with the first commemoration of the Armistice, which was declared a Public Holiday and the vast majority of businesses in the town closed for the day. A big parade led by bands set off at 10.00 am to arrive at a cenotaph ready for the now traditional silence, service and last post. As the parade marched past the Cenotaph the salute was taken by Lt General Sir Beauvoir de Lisle of Western Command. The parade set off again for a Drum Head Service which, because of the weather, had to be transferred from an open air service on the Caley Promenade to the Pier Pavilion. At the end of the service there was an address by Lt.-General Sir Beavoir de Lisle.

About 1,600 ex-servicemen had been identified and invited, of whom about 1,400 attended. Following the service they were allocated to various hotels in the area where they received an excellent meal. In the afternoon there were athletic sports, 6-a-side football, and a hockey competition. In the evening there was an entertaining Smoking Concert in a packed Pier Pavilion to which relatives of the fallen had also been invited. Tom would have enjoyed this day.

A programme containing full details of this day and other relevant documents can be found in the Conwy Archives in Llandudno.

During October the committee had received a specimen presentation wallet from a Walsall firm costing 3 shillings and 11 pence and they also offered a superior version to include the Council's coat of arms and gold block lettering that would cost 4s and 6d., or possibly 5s. The Council decided to purchase the superior wallets and distribute them to the ex-servicemen during the Armistice Day service and ceremonies on 11 November 1919, and each man was also presented with a Special Certificate. Tom's Certificate has not survived, but fortunately his wallet has survived. The Council's coat of arms is slightly faded but the inscription on the inside can still be seen clearly.

The inscription reads:

The residents of Colwyn Bay, Colwyn, and
District desire to record their high appreciation
of the loyal services rendered to King and
Country by you during the
Great War 1914 – 1919

This was made of lovely soft leather and there are signs of wear that indicate that Tom may have used this wallet regularly for the rest of his life.

The war also affected others in the family. It sounds bad for Tom that he was shot and then held in a prisoner-of-war camp, but he was lucky. Three days after he was taken prisoner, his cousin, David John Williams, was killed in action, aged twenty-nine.

David John was the son of Tom's uncle David. The two brothers had married two sisters so the relationship was particularly close. He joined the 2nd Battalion South Wales Borderers but his military records have not survived. He was probably involved in the battle of the Somme in 1916; the battalion suffered great losses there. Then they became involved in the battle of Cambrai in November 1917. On 3 December they came under heavy bombardment and then fierce fighting. Among the seventy-three men killed that day was Private 36119 David John Williams. He was killed only about ten miles from where Tom had been taken prisoner three days earlier.

During December 1917 two brothers living in Penmachno, about a mile and a half apart, received messages from the army. One was told his son Tom was missing; the other was told his son David John had been killed. This must have been devastating for the family but a situation that was unfortunately not uncommon for many families throughout Britain.

David John was buried at the Flesquieres Hill British Cemetery maintained by the Commonwealth Graves Commission and details can be seen on the Commission's website. Twenty-seven local men are named on the war memorial in Penmachno, including David John Williams.

David John's family lived in a terraced house called

" PRESWYLFA."

Er cof am fy nghyfaill David John Williams, Preswylfa,
Penmachno.   Yr hwn a laddwyd ar Faes y Frwydr
yn Ffraingc.

F. minor. (d Ab.)   M.C.   Rt. R. Thomas, Penmachno

Mor ddedwydd yw y rhai, trwy ffydd
  Sy'n myn'd o blith y byw,
Eu henwau'n perarogli sydd
  A'u hun mor dawel yw.

Ar ol eu holl flinderau dwys
  Gorphwyso maent mewn hedd,
Yn mhell o swn y byd a'i bwys
  Heb boen, yn llwch y bedd.

Llais un gorthrymydd byth ni ddaw
  I'w deffro i wylo mwy,
Na phrofedigaeth lem, na chroes
  Un loes ni theimlant hwy.

'Preswylfa' in Cwm Road, Penmachno. Robert Richard Thomas, a friend of David John, subsequently composed a hymn tune which he called 'Preswylfa', which was published in the November 1918 edition of *Y Cydymaith*, the quarterly publication of the Wesleyans in the Llanrwst district. The dedication in Welsh below the title is as follows:

> In memory of my friend David John Williams, Preswylfa, Penmachno. He was killed on the Field of Battle in France

Robert Richard Thomas was a quarryman and a fine musician. He was a cornet player and became the conductor of the Penmachno Band. He also conducted an adult choir and a children's choir. My mother remembered being a member of his children's choir. He was the father of Richie Thomas who became a very famous tenor and a member of the successful Penmachno concert party, 'Parti Penmachno'.

10

Other experiences in the POW camps

I had been undertaking research into conditions in the POW camps but I had a remarkable development as the book was being finalised. I also attended an interesting and highly informative meting which has helped me to better understand life inside the POW camps and the treatment of POWs in general.

Sergeant James Cunningham's War Diary

I had left messages on a number of the Rootsweb lists during 2010 and to my surprise I received one reply during February 2014! It was from a James Cunningham from Dunfermline who wondered whether the Jas Cunningham with the 13th Battalion Royal Scots, whose photo is on page 77, could be his grandfather. He was also in the 13th Bn. Royal Scots and was also a POW during WW1. The Royal Scots was the oldest Infantry Regiment in the British Army whose origins date back to 1633! Amongst the photographs in Tom's album there are three prisoners who were in the Royal Scots.

I sent James a copy of the photo but unfortunately it was not his grandfather. We exchanged emails and I sent him copies of some of the other photos taken in the POW camp. I found that his grandfather, also James Cunningham, was a Sergeant with the 13th Bn. Royal Scots and that he had kept a diary during his time in the POW Camp. I expressed great interest and James kindly sent me a copy of a transcription that he had made of his grandfather's diary and, with James' approval, I now summarise the contents of the diary as it gives a wonderful insight into the life of a POW.

Sgt. James Cunningham serving with the 13th Bn. Royal

Scots was taken prisoner on 21 March 1918 at Croisselles in Belgium. On the first night he slept in an open cage and was marched to a barracks in Marchinnes where he received his first food on 23 March which he described as disgusting. On 24 March one of the Royal Scots officers took everyone's names and promised he would write to let the regiment know that they were prisoners. One wonders how long it took for messages like this to get through to the British authorities and how long it then took for the messages to get through to the families. On 25 March they were moved into Germany and on 27 March they arrived at the Dulmen POW Camp and any money they had was taken and exchanged for "camp" money. On 29 March they were vaccinated and inoculated three times but, being so weak, many avoided this precautionary measure. But on Wednesday 3 April he records that they did receive their vaccinations.

As a Sergeant he was responsible for administrating food parcels and on 30 March he was put in charge of a hut of sixty men and received the first thirty emergency packets between sixty men. Over the next few days he describes the lack of food and starving and weak men. On 10 April he was moved into a different group where NCO's were separated from the men and he no longer had responsibility for a hut. On 18 April they left Dulmen and arrived at Limburg POW Camp on 19 April where bread rationing was twelve men to a loaf.

At Limburg many men went out working on farms every day. James knew that there had been an agreement between the British and German Governments that NCOs would not be required to work and refused all requests to do so fearing Court Martial at the end of the war. Some of the NCOs did volunteer but James stood firm despite repeated requests and threats. On 28 April he records, for the first time, that he had a bath.

They left Limburg Camp at 5.00 am on 1 May and eventually arrived at the Parchim POW Camp at 6.00 am on 3 May. Here he describes the lack of food and, when received, its poor quality; a bath without soap or towel and attending a Church Service. He also mentions sending a card home. They left Parchim on 13 May and arrived at Springhirsch POW Camp for NCOs on 14 May. Springhirsch, near to Lentfohrden, is a district of Nutzen to the north of Hamburg. Again he records the lack of and poor quality of the food and he records an examination by a Medical Officer on 19 May as a farce.

He records that they were required to undertake exercise between 9.00 am and 11.00 am each day with a fifteen-minute break. On 21 May the fifteen-minute break was withdrawn because the Camp Authorities considered that they hadn't marched round quickly enough. On 24 May the names of fifty men who ignored the order not to take the fifteen-minute break were taken and on 29 May these fifty men were put into prison. It's not recorded how long these men spent in prison. More men were being sent to this camp and on 1 June he records 700 men in camp. Despite his comments on the food he says on 4 June that as this was an NCOs' Camp that the food is better than at others, but he adds that as the number of prisoners increased that it was getting worse.

On 1 July he states that at his previous camps the Russians did all the cooking and the feeling was that they were robbing the others of their rations. In this camp the British did the cooking and they were considered to be cleaner but the rest of the men still considered that they were being robbed! On 7 July he sent a card 'to Copenhagen' to say that he was not in receipt of any bread. Would this have been to the Red Cross or other humanitarian organisation? On 14 October he records that he received "Copenhagen biscuits" and this is the only other reference to Copenhagen.

During July he records lack of food, baths without soap, attending church services and sending postcards home. On 10 July a further 540 men arrived at camp with further numbers during August and by 7 September there were 1,476 prisoners in the camp. All the additional arrivals put further pressure on the food supply. There's an interesting note on 4 August saying that he's sent a card home asking for his family to send 'money and baccy'. On 6 August he says that he went 'round the old hands begging their mouldy bread which they couldn't eat themselves'. This suggests that those POWs who had been there longer were getting supplies but that the newer ones were not. It also suggests that by the time they received it that is was old and got mouldy before they could finish eating it.

On 15 August, for the first time, there is mention that 1,265 packets came to the Camp and on 25 August a further 2,364 packets were delivered. On 27 August James was delighted to have received his packet containing, groceries, tobacco and biscuits. Further deliveries of packets are reported on 30 August, 9, 17, 23 and 30 September. On 14 September he reports his first bath with soap and again on 20 September. The entry on 3 October is 'Sanitary inspector visited the camp and found numerable complaints against the Germans' but there is no record that anything happened as a result of these complaints.

During October and November there are mentions of packages arriving at the camp and these are clearly very important events in the lives of the prisoners. On 17 October there is the first mention of rumours of peace and these are repeated on 25 and 29 October. On 6 November they heard that the Germans had agreed to terms for an armistice and on 8 November they heard that the armistice had actually begun and the Germans changed their attitude towards them. There were no parades on 9, 10, 11 and 12 November but strangely there is no mention that they knew that the Armistice had been signed on 11 November.

On 13 November the Sergeant Majors were allowed to go outside the camp for the first time without escorts. On 15 November they were told that the British navy was expected to arrive in Kiel any minute and on 18 November the gates were opened to allow anyone to go out at any time. On 20 November James records, 'This was the best day I had since I left home, five of us went to Barmstedt and Kaltenkirchen and dined in a German's house'.

Clothes were distributed on 21 November and he went out again on 22 November. On 23 November he records that there are strong rumours that they will setting off for home on certain dates but that they were being continually disappointed. He writes, 'I may say those few weeks passed slower than the former months of my internment.' I'm not surprised; the anxiety of waiting to go home must have been intense. He also notes that a letter from an aunt arrived that day dated six months earlier on 24 June! It was his first letter for twelve weeks.

On 24 November a notice was put up in the camp to say that the rumours about prisoners leaving Hamburg for home were not true and any man attempting to reach Hamburg on his own would delay the release for others. On 25 November James and some friends went for a 21km walk and said he felt himself getting stronger every day. A notice put up on 25 November said that it was possible that they could be leaving Germany within two weeks, which cheered everyone up. On 28 November he and some friends went on a 33 km round trip walk to Barmstedt but on the way back he was taken ill; he thought that he would never finish the walk. He eventually arrived back and went straight to bed where he remained for three days suffering a severe dose of influenza. Despite the lack of food, this is the first time in the diary when he states that he was unwell. He is in bed on 29 and 30 November but on 1 December he states that he is "up and feeling in the pink but not near rid of the cold".

On 2 December he walks with friends to Barmstedt again and they each sell a simmet which a Scottish word for a long vest. One received 30 marks for his and James and his friend received 45 marks for their two so they now had some spending money. His friends go off to Hamburg on 3 December for a couple of nights but James doesn't feel up to it. On 8 December James and his friends go to Hamburg overnight, enjoyed the sights on the 9th but went back to the camp for rations on the 10th. They went back to Hamburg on the 11th and stayed "in private digs at 6 marks per week". They enjoyed themselves on the 12th and on the 13th he purchased an Iron Cross from a German widow, which his grandson still has. This illustrates the desperate situation of many of the German civilians. They later received a phone message to get back as the camp was moving.

They returned on the 14th and on 15 December they got on the train for Warnamunde and arrived at the docks the following morning to set sail for Denmark. They arrived at Waarhus at 8.00 am on 17 December to a great welcome from the Danish and set off by train to arrive at camp at 12.30 pm. They were inspected by a Major from the British Army for the first time and told they would leave for home at the earliest opportunity. They were still there on 21 December when they got paid 70 Kroners per man and received a good bath and a change of clothing.

They left the camp at 5.00 pm on 23 December, embarked on board ship, the SS CPA Koch, at 11.00 pm and set sail for Leith at 2.00 am. They were fitted out with khaki on board and issued with new kit on the 24th and they were still at sea on Christmas Day when nearly everyone on board was seasick! The ship arrived at Leith at 9.00 am on 26 December and they disembarked at 11.00 am to a great reception. This was over six weeks after the Armistice was signed and by 12 noon they set off by train to Ripon to the POW Reception Camp.

I was delighted to have received a copy of this diary which gave me an insight to life in a POW camp, and what happened between the date the Armistice was signed and the date they arrived home in Britain. Tom's experiences would not have been identical to James' but there would clearly have been some similarities.

James does not unfortunately have a photo of his grandfather in uniform but a photo of him in civilian clothes taken around 1924 is shown. James Cunningham joined the Army Reserves in 1910 and later joined the 13th Battalion

Royal Scots. During WW1 the number of battalions in the Royal Scots increased to thirty-five, of which fifteen battalions served as active first line units and amongst these was the 13th Battalion. In March 2006 the Royal Scots merged with other Scottish Infantry Regiments to form The Royal Regiment of Scotland.

Former Sergeant James Cunningham

The Western Front Association

The Western Front Association (WFA) was formed in 1980 with the aim of furthering interest in The Great War and has numerous branches throughout the country most of whom have monthly meetings. I looked at their events programme in January 2014 and found that only two out of numerous advertised monthly events dealt with the experience of prisoners during the war. I attended one of the meetings of the Birmingham Branch where I learnt much from a most interesting and informative talk by Richard Lloyd who has done considerable research into POWs and had interviewed a number of surviving POWs during the 1970s.

Much of Richard's talk confirmed what was included in James Cunningham's War Diary. Not only did new POWs initially have to spend time in an open cage but many had to construct their own cages! Many were escorted by German troops on horseback and when they stopped for food, they had to use their helmets to receive soup. They were taken to camps on trains in cattle trucks and Scottish POWs were subjected to ridicule for the wearing the kilt. Their trains would stop at every station so that they could be displayed to the civilian population as men dressed as women. I hope that Tom was not subjected to this humiliation. As he was injured I assume that he was taken initially to a hospital for treatment and there is a possibility that he was not taken to the camp in the company of other kilted prisoners.

There are tales of how the German Red Cross would take water to a train carrying POWs, offer them water and then pour it on the floor in front of them! The Russians were worse off in the camps as they received no rations from home. This could explain why Tom had so many photos of Russians. They could be selling their photos in order to buy food or to exchange for food.

One of the most disturbing aspects was that a number of

prisoners never made it to an official POW Camp. These men were simply used as slave labour and they were never recorded as prisoners. Very little is known about these men who became the 'forgotten prisoners'.

Richard explained that most of the prisoners who were working were living and sleeping at their employers' premises and not at the camp where they were registered. This is confirmed by a declaration issued from Berlin following the armistice to state what was to happen to working POWs billeted outside the camp:

The Treatment of Prisoners of War

1. Prisoners of War are to remain at their place of work.
2. Prisoners of War will receive from today onwards equal pay with free German workmen.
3. They are not bound to work but may do so at their own desire.
4. The employer is still bound to keep to the agreements concluded.
5. Troops guarding Prisoners of War will now unload rifles.
6. After working hours all Prisoners of War will remain in the buildings provided for their shelter.
7. The employer is still bound to feed all Prisoners of War.
8. Notice will be sent when Prisoners of War are to be returned to their respective camps.

(Signed)
Wolf Kretschmer
Executive Committee
Berlin
11 November 1918

One of the ex-POWs Richard met during the 1970s was a Private William Brunsall who had been a prisoner at the Cassel POW Camp. He gave Richard a leaflet which was given to each POW when they left that camp for repatriation to the United Kingdom. This is reproduced below with Richard's permission:

Gentlemen,

The war is over? A little while – and you will see your native land again, your homes, your loved ones, your friends, and you will once more take up your accustomed work.

The fortune of war brought you as prisoners into our hands. You were freed, even against your own will, from the fighting, from danger and from death. But the joys of peace were not yours, for there was no peace. Now peace is coming, and peace means liberty. When you are already reunited to your families, thousands of our countrymen will still be pining in far off prison camps with hearts as hungry for home as yours.

You have suffered in confinement – as who would not? It was the fate of every prisoner in every prison-camp in the world to eat his heart out with longing, to chafe against the loss of liberty, to suffer from home sickness, brooding, discouragement, black despair. The days, the weeks, the weary years crept by, and there was no end in sight. There were many misunderstandings, discomforts and irritations.

Your situation has been a difficult one. Our own has been desperate. Our country blockaded, our civil population and army suffering from want of proper sufficient food and materials, the enormous demands made upon our harassed land from every side – these and many other afflictions made it impossible to do all that we should liked to have done. Under the circumstances we did our best to lessen the hardships of your lot, to ensure you comfort, to provide you with pastime, employment, mental and bodily recreation. It is not likely that you will know how difficult our circumstances have been.

We know that errors have been committed and that there have been hardships for which the former system was to blame. There have been wrongs and evils on both sides. We hope that you will always think of that – and be just.

You entered the old empire of Germany; you leave the new Republic, the newest and, as we hope to make it, the freest land in the world. We are sorry that you saw little of what we are proud of in the former Germany – our arts, our sciences, our model cities, our theatres, our schools, industries, our social institutions, as well as the real beauty of our scenery and the real soul of our people, akin to many things to your own.

But these things will remain part of the new Germany. Once the barriers of artificial hatred and misunderstanding have fallen, we hope that you will learn to know that in happier times, these grander features of our land whose unwilling guests you have been. A barbed wire enclosure is not the proper way to survey or judge a great nation.

The war has blinded all nations. But if a true and just peace will result in opening the eyes of the peoples to the fact that their interests are common – that no difference in flags, government, speech or nationality can alter the great truth of the fraternity of all men, this war will not have been fought in vain. If the peoples at last realise that it is not each other who are the enemies, but the ruthless forces of Imperialism and Capitalism, of Militarism of all sorts, of jingo Journalism that sows falsehood, hatred and suspicion, then this war will not have been fought in vain. Then peace will not have been established in vain.

We hope that every one of you will go home carrying a message of good will, of conciliation, of enlightenment. Let all men go forth as missionaries of the new evangel, as interpreters between nation and nation.

The valiant dead who once fought against each other have long been sleeping as comrades side by side in the same earth. May the living who once fought against each other labour as comrades side by side upon this self-same earth.

This is the message with which we bid you farewell.

Cassel,
Germany,
December 1918

Readers can judge whether this was a cynical attempt by the German authorities to justify the actions during the war or whether it was a genuine message of regret for past actions and hope and good will for a new world in the future. We now know, of course, that unfortunately the excellent hopes expressed in the last paragraphs were not fulfilled, and Europe and the world drifted into another disastrous war in just over twenty years following the Peace Treaty of 28 June 1919.

11
1918-1945
After the War

Since leaving the POW Reception Camp in Ripon at the end of December 1918 Tom had been on leave until he started working again at H R Davies, Abergele Road, Colwyn Bay on 26 March 1919. He'd spent most of his leave period in Colwyn Bay with some time with his family in Penmachno. He'd therefore had time to meet his friends and work colleagues in Colwyn Bay and he must have been ready to start work again but the one aspect for which I've no information is whether his injuries affected his work.

Tom on his motorbike, post-war, on his tour of England

There are two postcards from Colwyn Bay dated 6 June and 31 July to my mother saying that he would be coming to Penmachno on Saturday so presumably the visits to his family continued as they did before the war. There are very few postcards during the rest of 1919 or during 1920.

In the photo album there's an undated photo of Tom looking smart on a motorbike, which he certainly had by the summer of 1921 as the message on the back of the postcard from Oxford reads: 'Here today, starting for Brighton. Had a good journey without any problems through Shrewsbury, Hereford, Monmouth, through the Wye Valley to Gloucester'. This card was dated 1 August 1921. This was quite a journey and I assumed he'd stayed overnight in Oxford until I noticed the time on the date stamp is 6.30 pm. It was therefore quite possible that he was doing the whole journey from Colwyn Bay to Brighton in one day unless he had stayed in Oswestry or Shrewsbury the previous night. Presumably he stayed in Brighton that night.

The next postcard is from London dated 4 August 1921 timed at 12.45 pm. The message reads: 'Here since Wednesday. Starting today for Birmingham. Rain here yesterday.' He had therefore spent 4 nights in Brighton and London, and now was off to Birmingham. He had certainly not lost his desire to travel but now he was doing it on his motorbike.

Tom's father died on 9 February 1922. Tom must have been at the funeral but there are no postcards. The next card is from London dated 9 August 1922. The message reads: 'I'm very sorry that I didn't send anything earlier. I'm still keeping going.' It sounds as this was as long a journey as that in the previous year.

There is a card sent to Tom in May 1919 care of a Mrs Cooper, Greenfield Road, Colwyn Bay and on 15 March 1924 there is a card from Tom showing a photo of Greenfield Road. On the back he says that half of Trevor House can be seen on the right of this photo. So this is where Tom settled down to live on his return from the war.

The next photo shows my mother and a friend on the back of Tom's motorbike. The date on the back is 1929 and my mother, sitting on the back, is now aged twenty, and the girl at the front is Cissie Williams who became a teacher and was one of my teachers at the Penmachno Primary School during the early 1940s. The photo is taken at Bod Hyfryd, an end terrace house in Cwm Road, Penmachno, where Cissie lived and where I spent many happy hours during the 1940s.

Greenfield Road in Colwyn Bay, where Tom settled after the War

A number of photos in Tom's Album are of theatrical characters but unfortunately there are only two with a name on them. The back of the first photo is a message dated May

Kate (pillion) and friend on Tom's bike, 1929

1920 from J. O. Davies stating that he is playing the character of Messenger in *Blodwen*. This would be the operetta *Hywel a Blodwen* originally written in Welsh and composed by the famous composer Joseph Parry. The second of these photos clearly states that the group is the Colwyn Bay Light Opera Company' and their production in 1927 is *Belle of Brittany*. Mr J. O. Davies is playing *Poquelin* and he has signed the photo. A copy of the programme for this poduction can be seen at the Conwy

Archives, Llandudno. Tom is clearly friends with people in the company but there is no suggestion that he participated as a performer. Perhaps he used his tailoring skills to help with the costumes.

The most interesting photo is an autographed photo of England cricketer S .F. Barnes. Sidney Barnes was the first player to have been picked for England directly from the Lancashire League and played in twenty-seven Tests between 1901 and 1914, taking 189 wickets at an average of 16.43 runs each. But what was his photo doing in Tom's album? Was he living in Colwyn Bay?

Sidney Barnes

I was surprised to discover that there was a Wales cricket team which played sixteen first-class matches between 1923 and 1930. Sidney Barnes, then in his fifties, played in nine of these matches between 1927 and 1930, taking forty-nine wickets. These included an eight-wicket win over the West Indies at Llandudno in 1928, when Barnes took seven wickets for fifty-one runs. But how was Sidney Barnes qualified to play for Wales?

The Colwyn Bay Cricket ground at Rhos-on-Sea was established in 1924. Sidney Barnes lived in the area and acted as a coach in the late 1920s so he therefore became eligible to play for Wales. He also played for North Wales and played his last match, North Wales versus an Empire XI, in 1942 at the age of sixty-nine! Tom could well have been a cricket fan and could have met Barnes at the cricket ground, or Barnes could have brought a suit from Tom at H. R. Davies.

The last photo shows Tom in his late fifties standing on the promenade in Colwyn Bay and this is how I remember him. I probably met him when I was younger but the one meeting that sticks in my memory was when he came to visit us at Gwiga probably during the summer of 1945 when I was approaching my seventh birthday. Having heard my mother talk so much about her Uncle Tom I was full of anticipation and had climbed a tree as a look-out to await his coming. The vision of him walking across the fields towards the farm house is still in my mind and as he got nearer he started waving. I was really excited and ran back into the house to tell them that Tom was on his way. I can't remember much else but I know that I thoroughly enjoyed the day. On 3 September my mother and I were back living in Liverpool and on 18 September 1945 Tom sadly died at the age of fifty-nine. He had problems with his coronary arteries, and his death must have been sudden and unexpected as his Death Certificate is signed by a Coroner following a post-mortem.

Tom on the Colwyn Bay prom, not long before his death in 1945 at the age of fifty-nine

He was buried on 21 September in the New Cemetery, Cwm Road, Penmachno now called the Arwelfa Cemetery and six of his fellow workers at H. R. Davies were coffin bearers. A tribute to him published in *Yr Herald Cymraeg* says that he was affectionately known as 'Tom Bach y Gwiga' to his contemporaries in the village and describes him as a unique character full of humour. The writer had spent many happy hours in his company and had never heard him speak badly of anyone and describes him as a true Christian. It was these qualities that enabled him to cope with the horrors of the Great War and life in the POW camps, where he made friends with his fellow prisoners from various nationalities.

My mother gave Tom's Liverpool Scottish kilt to his cousin Hugh (brother of David John Williams killed in 1917) who was also a tailor. He used it to make a coat for his disabled son which was very useful in the days of rationing in 1945.

Everyone who knew Tom spoke highly of him. My mother's second cousin Nell Jones (a niece of David John Williams) told me that whenever they went to Colwyn Bay as children they would always go to see Tom in the shop and he would give them half a crown to spend. My mother clearly thought the world of her Uncle Tom and I wish I had known him but I'm thoroughly grateful to my grandmother, and my mother, for keeping his photo album and all the postcards safely so that I could get some idea of his life. I also give special thanks to my sister, Iola Owen, who undertook the enormous task of cataloguing the postcards.

Further Reading

The Liverpool Scottish, 1900-1919, Major A. M. McGilchrist, published 1930, and republished by The Naval & Military Press (2011). Detailed account of the activities of the Liverpool Scottish during the Great War.

www.liverpoolscottish.org.uk for details of activities and contact details, and visiting the Archives.

Cambrai 1917: The Myth of the First Great Tank Battle, Bryn Hammond (Phoenix).

Cambrai 1917: The birth of armoured warfare, Alexander Turner and Peter Dennis (Osprey Publishing).

The Prisoner of War in Germany, Daniel J MacCarthy, published in 1918, see https://archive.org

Websites

The Long, Long Trail: Excellent source of information: *www.1914-18.net*

The Western Front Association has branches which hold regular events throughout the country. Website, *www.westernfrontassociation.com,* is full of useful and interesting information.

Individual War Records: the 30 per cent that have survived are on microfilm at the National Archives in Kew but they are now available on websites such as *www.ancestry.co.uk*

Regimental Museums/Archives. Google the name of the regiment to find a museum/archive. You can obtain information and extracts from their War Diary.

The County Archives for the area where your ancestor lived just before and after the War will have records that could be relevant. Check their website.

Local newspapers of the period will contain reports of interest. Try the local County Archives; many can now be found on websites such as the National Library of Wales (*www.llgc.org.uk*) or the British Library (*britishnewspaperarchive.co.uk*)

Commonwealth War Graves Commission, www.cwgc.org. Much helpful information, including the Certificate for those buried in the cemeteries, and a photograph of the cemetery.

The Great War Forum, *http://1914-18invasionzone.com/forums/*: numerous forums covering the whole range of military activity during this period, including a forum on POWs.

Rootsweb Messaging lists are used by family history researchers to find information about their ancestors. Go to *www.rootsweb.ancestry.com* . Look under 'Mailing Lists' and click 'Index' to find a huge list. Go to 'International' and amongst the countries of the world you'll find England, Northern Ireland, Scotland and Wales. Go to 'Wales', for example, and find lists based on the traditional counties. It's free to subscribe to these lists and you will then receive copies of the messages being sent to the list. You can send your message and wait for any response.

Other useful websites include:
www.nationalarchives.gov.uk
www.warmemorialsonline.org.uk
https://livesofthefirstworldwar.org
www.jisc.ac.uk (teaching resources)
www.cymruncofio.org (Wales Remembers)
www.cymruww1.llgc.org.uk (National Library of Wales)